YANKEE
HILL-COUNTRY
COOKING

Heirloom Recipes from
Rural Kitchens

by

BEATRICE VAUGHAN

GRAMERCY PUBLISHING COMPANY
NEW YORK

DEDICATED TO
THE MEMORY OF MY MOTHER
AND ALL OTHER GOOD COOKS
OF THE HILL COUNTRY

ACKNOWLEDGMENTS

I wish it were possible to thank individually the women
who passed on to me treasured family recipes. Especially
am I indebted to Mildred Cook and Emma Coombs,
and I deeply regret that those good friends did not live
to see this book a reality. And my warm gratitude to
Weston Cate, Jr., without whose help and encourage-
ment at the beginning this book might never have
been written, and to Marvin Midgette and James
Wechsler of *The Valley News* for the many ways in
which they have helped me.   B.V.

Copyright © MCMLXIII by Beatrice Vaughan
Library of Congress Catalog Card Number: 63-13862
All rights reserved.
This edition is published by
Gramercy Publishing Company
a division of Crown Publishers, Inc.
by arrangement with The Stephen Greene Press
a   b   c   d   e   f   g   h
Manufactured in the United States of America

Contents

Translations

MY BIGGEST PROBLEM in preparing this book has been to present the old recipes in terms that would make them most usable by the space-age housewife without, however, sacrificing their basic simplicity. Many I amplified as I set them down, for they were written in almost telegraphic form by experienced cooks who assumed that other housewives could fill in any gaps as to ingredients and methods. Still, there are some general points that can do with a bit of translation—and here they are.

BAKING SODA is familiar bicarbonate of soda, and was called for in the old rules either to act as a leavening agent in baking, or to prevent curdling of milk-and-tomato dishes, or to provide an aerated texture to such confections as brittle candies.

Commercial baking powders as we know them are fairly modern conveniences. Until the mid-1800s the housewife in Yankee hill country relied on baking soda—elegantly called "saleratus" —combined with the acidity of buttermilk and sour milk or cream, or such sweeteners as molasses, etc., for making quick breads. A number of receipts using baking soda are still in demand, though, because of the tender crumb and delicate flavor imparted, and which combination products used with sweet milk can't duplicate.

SOUR MILK and CREAM were natural and

staple ingredients in the old days, and butter-milk came right from the churn after the golden grains of butter had "gathered"—but no longer. Pasteurization prevents the natural "clabbering" of milk or cream, so when old-fashioned thick sour milk is called for, merely use commercially cultured buttermilk from the dairy case of your supermarket; the same source offers commer-cially soured cream.

Of course if you have access to certified raw milk, you can boost the souring process by add-ing 1 tablespoon of vinegar or lemon juice to each 1 cup of this sweet milk, and letting it stand at room temperature until it curdles properly.

SPIDERS are cherished items in my kitchen equipment, yet many a young bride looks a-skance when I mention them—but her face clears happily when I explain that a spider is nothing more mysterious than a capacious frying pan, preferably of cast iron, in which things fry or simmer or keep warm in a wonderfully satisfac-tory manner.

STORE CHEESE is old-style wheel cheddar, fairly crumbly, and ranging from almost mild to very sharp indeed—and is not to be confused with the so-called process cheeses. It can be found in every New England country store and can be bought in any amount. I prefer it both for table use and for cooking. However, the average suppermarket's pre-cut cheddar will answer very well for these recipes.

MAPLE SUGAR produced commercially in blocks today is softer and wetter than the old tub or cake sugar in use when these recipes were evolved. Therefore I've included the approximate weight required to furnish the measurement called for: a "good ¼ pound" is nearer 5 ounces than 4—and so on. Amounts of maple syrup I've not translated, since syrup hasn't changed much in the last half-century except for having more delicate color and flavor now as the result of improved equipment.

BACK OF THE STOVE is an expression held over from our yesterdays, when it was taken for granted that cooks used huge black-iron wood ranges, with plenty of space away from the firebox to let things finish cooking slowly and oh-so-gently. Lucky the cook who still owns such a stove! No problem for her to keep foods warm until served—on the high shelf by the stovepipe, or in the warming oven (ideal for drying mittens between meals, too), or in the oven whose door is propped open.

With a little maneuvering with double boilers and trivets, though, it's possible to achieve the same slow-cooking or warming results on a modern gas or electric stove.

CHAPTER ONE

Soups, Stews and Chowders

THE EARLY HOUSEWIFE of our hill country depended upon her capacious black iron soup kettle to serve her family hearty meals that would stick to their ribs and at the same time utilize every scrap of meat or vegetables, every bit of goodness from bones and leftover pan-gravy. Nothing is easier to make without great expense than a good soup, and soups seem to lend themselves to variation and experiment—an ingredient casually added or omitted, more of this or less of that; and perhaps the result will be a subtle new combination to be repeated intentionally next time.

In addition to the well-known salting and drying, our forebears relied on freezing to preserve food to an extent that would astonish many people today who think of food-freezing as a modern innovation. My own great-grandmother froze her soup as one way of stock-

1

piling food for the Winter. As soon as the weather was really cold she made a huge kettleful of meat and vegetable soup. When it had simmered down to the right concentration, the widemouthed kettle was set in the frigid back pantry, which was almost as cold as all outdoors. In the center of the kettle she stood upright a wooden paddle having a hole in the end of its handle. When the soup had frozen to granite hardness, great-grandmother warmed the outside of the kettle just enough to slide the icy lump out intact. The frozen mass was hung by slipping the hole in the handle over a nail in a high beam. When soup was needed, she merely chopped off a hunk with the hatchet and heated it with the requisite amount of water.

Tomato Cream Soup

4 cups canned tomatoes, undrained
1 medium onion, peeled and chopped
2 stalks celery, chopped fine
4 cups milk, scalded
about 1 tablespoon flour for thickening
½ teaspoon baking soda
1 tablespoon butter
salt and pepper to taste

Simmer tomatoes, onion and celery for 30 minutes. Meanwhile scald milk and thicken slightly with the flour mixed with a little water to make a paste. Just before serving, add soda to tomatoes and as frothing subsides, strain into hot milk, stirring constantly (the soda prevents curdling). Add butter, then salt and pepper to taste. Serve at once. Will serve 5 to 6.

This recipe may be doubled but *do not* increase the amount of soda.

Potato Soup

6 medium potatoes, peeled and quartered
2 large onions, peeled and quartered
6 celery stalks, untrimmed, cubed
1 teaspoon salt
about 4 cups milk
1 tablespoon butter
salt and pepper to taste

Put potatoes, onions and celery in water just covering, add 1 teaspoon salt and simmer until very tender. Remove from heat and rub vegetables in their liquor through a sieve. Add milk until soup is desired consistency and return to low heat. Add butter, then salt and pepper to taste. Soup will thicken as it stands and more milk may be added. Will serve 5 to 6.

Salt Cod Chowder

½ pound salt codfish, freshened
3 ¼-inch slices salt pork, diced
4 medium potatoes, peeled and diced
2 medium onions, peeled and diced
6 cups milk
salt and pepper to taste

Freshen codfish by soaking in cold water for several hours, preferably overnight, then pick apart carefully. Fry salt pork gently in the heavy kettle you are to use. When golden brown, add potatoes, onions and codfish. Simmer gently in as little water as possible for about 20 minutes or until all is very tender. Then add milk and salt and pepper to taste. Heat very hot and serve. Serves 5 to 6.

Quick Vegetable Chowder

3 tablespoons butter
1 medium onion, peeled and chopped
1 pint canned string beans, drained
1 pint canned tomatoes, undrained
1 pint canned cream-style corn
¼ teaspoon baking soda
1 pint milk, scalded
salt and pepper to taste

Melt butter in bottom of heavy kettle. Add onion and cook slowly for about 5 minutes. Add beans, corn and tomatoes. Heat all very hot, then add soda (to prevent curdling). As frothing subsides, add milk slowly, stirring well. Season to taste with salt and pepper and serve at once. Will serve 4 to 5.

Salmon Chowder

1   tall can salmon
3 medium potatoes, peeled and sliced thin
2 cups boiling water
½ teaspoon salt
2 tablespoons butter
2 medium onions, peeled and chopped fine
3 tablespoons flour
pinch of pepper
3 cups milk

Add the salt to the boiling water. Cook potatoes until tender in the boiling water. Melt butter in bottom of heavy kettle, add onions and cook gently until tender. Stir in flour and pepper, then add the potatoes with their boiling water. Simmer all together for about 15 minutes. Remove skin and bones from salmon and add. Add milk, bring to boiling point and serve. Will serve 6.

Baked Bean Soup

4 cups leftover baked beans, liquid and all
4 cups water
1 large onion, peeled and quartered
4 cups canned tomatoes, undrained
1 tablespoon butter
salt and pepper to taste

Put beans, onion and water into kettle and simmer slowly for 1 hour. Remove from heat and rub all, with water, through sieve. Return to kettle, add tomatoes to bean mixture and simmer 1 hour longer. Season to taste with salt and pepper and add butter. Will serve 6 to 8. This soup is excellent warmed up the second day.

Fish Chowder

about 1½ pounds fresh haddock or cod
3 cups water
1 teaspoon salt
3 ¼-inch slices fat salt pork, diced
3 medium potatoes, peeled and diced
2 medium onions, peeled and diced
4 cups milk
1 tablespoon butter
salt and pepper to taste

Put fish in kettle, add 3 cups water and 1 teaspoon salt. Poach slowly until fish can be pulled apart with fork, but not so much that it gets mushy. Remove from water, saving the water to boil potatoes in. Boil potatoes until tender. While potatoes are cooking, fry salt pork in a small frying pan until golden brown, add diced onions and cook slowly for 5 minutes longer. Remove skin and bones from fish, which is now cool enough to handle easily. To the kettle of undrained cooked potatoes, add the fish, then add pork and onions with the fat from the frying pan. Add milk. Let come just to boiling point, add the butter, then pepper and salt to taste. Will serve 6.

Tomato Corn Chowder

4 cups canned tomatoes, undrained

4 cups canned cream-style corn

¼ teaspoon baking soda

3 ¼-inch slices fat salt pork, diced

1 medium onion, peeled and diced

3 medium potatoes, peeled and diced

1 teaspoon salt

6 cups hot milk

pinch of pepper

Fry salt pork in heavy kettle until golden brown, add onion and continue cooking for 5 minutes more. Boil potatoes until tender in just enough water to cover, adding the teaspoon of salt. Do not drain, but add salt pork and onion, with the fat from the frying pan. Then add corn and tomatoes. Heat very hot and add soda. When frothing subsides, add hot milk. Season with pepper and a little more salt if desired. Will serve 6.

Green Pea and Tomato Soup

2½ cups green peas, fresh or frozen
2½ cups canned tomatoes, undrained
1 small onion, peeled and diced
1 cup water
2 tablespoons butter, melted
2 tablespoons flour
¼ teaspoon baking soda
3 cups milk, scalded
salt and pepper to taste

Simmer peas, tomatoes and onion in the 1 cup water until peas are very tender. Remove from fire and rub all, with the liquid, through a sieve. Return to heat and thicken with paste made from melted butter and flour, stirring well. Add soda (to prevent curdling), then when froth dies down add scalded milk. Season to taste with salt and pepper. Serve at once. Will serve 6.

Parsnip Stew

4 ¼-inch slices salt pork, diced
1 medium onion, peeled and chopped
1½ cups peeled and diced parsnips
2 medium potatoes, peeled and diced
2 cups boiling water
1 teaspoon salt
pinch of pepper
4 cups milk, scalded
1 tablespoon butter

In the bottom of heavy kettle, fry salt pork gently until golden brown. Add onion and continue cooking for 5 minutes longer. Add parsnips, potatoes, boiling water, salt and pepper. Simmer until all is very tender, about 30 minutes. Add hot milk and butter, heat very hot and serve. Will serve 6 to 8.

Vegetable Oyster Stew

2 bunches salsify root (oyster plant)
½ teaspoon salt
water
about 5 cups milk
2 tablespoons butter
salt and pepper to taste

Wash and scrape salsify root and cut in ¼-inch slices. Barely cover with water to which the ½ teaspoon salt has been added. Simmer until very tender, about 25 minutes. Do not drain, but add hot milk as desired. Add butter, then salt and pepper to taste. Bring just to boiling point and serve with oyster crackers. Serves 4 to 5.

This stew improves if left to blend over very low heat for about 1 hour, but be sure it does not boil. This really does taste like oyster stew and can be served to those who love the taste of seafood but are allergic to shellfish.

CHAPTER TWO

Eggs and Cheese

MOST HILL FARMS in olden days had rather haphazard poultry flocks, and the supply of eggs was equally so. In the Spring, when every hen seemed bent on motherhood, we children were expected to play a sort of hide-and-seek game of finding stolen nests and gathering the precious eggs while they were still fresh. To make sure of their freshness, the eggs were tested by lowering them into a pan of cold water. If they floated they were promptly discarded.

We had quantities of eggs all Fall until Winter settled down to steady near-zero cold; then we had none at all. When eggs were plentiful we ate them in all sorts of ways, but when they were scarce my mother had a hard time finding one to use in a cake. This seasonal dearth was responsible, I am sure, for the great number of recipes in old notebooks for two-egg angel cake, or one-egg sponge cake, as well as for eggless muffins, doughnuts and cookies.

Year round, however, all good farmwives had a plentiful supply of cottage cheese—called by the old names of pot or Dutch cheese. A big bowl of this delicious, crumbly white cheese was almost as indispensable at dinner time as the salt and pepper, and it was often used in cooking.

Even then few farmers made their own yellow cheese, but this robust cheddar was well known as "store cheese" because there was always a huge wheel of it down at the village store, more or less protected by a cracked glass dome and with an enormous cleaver close by, ready for the proprietor to slice off a pound or so for anyone whose grocery money ran to the expenditure.

Potatoes, Salt Cod and Eggs

½ pound salt codfish, freshened
whole new potatoes to serve 6
4 eggs, hard boiled
about 2 cups cream
2 tablespoons butter
salt and pepper to taste

Soak codfish overnight in water to freshen. Pick apart into small pieces. Scrub small new potatoes until peels have disappeared. Cook fish and potatoes together in unsalted water until tender, drain well and return to kettle. Pour cream over fish and potatoes, making sure each potato has been moistened. Add sliced hard-boiled eggs, butter, and season to taste with salt and pepper.

Then: "Let stand on back of stove until cream has almost all been absorbed," my old rule says. In today's language this means to keep the kettle warm *but not over the heat* while other dishes for the meal are being prepared. Just before serving, heat carefully until very hot and serve at once. Will serve 6.

This is one of my oldest recipes, and there are no set amounts for the ingredients. Old potatoes may be used, of course, but new ones are preferable.

Baked Stuffed Eggs

    9 hard-boiled eggs
    6 tablespoons butter
    1 teaspoon grated onion
    1½ teaspoons prepared mustard
    ½ teaspoon salt
    pinch of pepper
    1 cup sour cream
    ½ cup dry breadcrumbs

Peel eggs and cut in half lengthwise. Remove yolks and mash, mixing with 3 tablespoons of the butter, which has been softened, then adding the onion, mustard, salt and pepper. Fill egg whites with this mixture and place in buttered baking dish, cut side down. Cover with the sour cream. Melt the remaining 3 tablespoons of butter and mix with the breadcrumbs; sprinkle over eggs. Bake in 350 oven for about 30 minutes. Will serve 5 to 6.

Eggs in Mashed Potato Nests

about 4 cups mashed potatoes
7 eggs
3 tablespoons butter, melted
salt and pepper to taste
12 small strips bacon, partially cooked

Beat 1 whole egg, then blend with melted butter into mashed potatoes, with salt and pepper to taste. Beat until light and fluffy. Fill a buttered, deep pie plate with the potato mixture, smoothing the top flat. Make six depressions in the mixture with the back of a spoon, and break 1 egg into each depression. Lay the strips of partially cooked bacon over all. Bake in 400 oven until eggs are set and bacon crisp. Will serve 6.

Either leftover or freshly mashed potatoes may be used.

Scrambled Eggs with Sour Cream

8 eggs, large
about ½ cup sour cream
2 tablespoons butter
salt and pepper to taste

Scramble the eggs according to your favorite method. The amounts given above serve 4 in my family, and are arrived at by substituting sour cream for the same amount of sweet cream or milk I'd otherwise use.

I inherited from a long line of farmwives my taste for sour cream as a flavoring ingredient for sauces, gravies—and eggs. How much you use will depend on the tastes of your family.

Cheese Bread Soufflé

4 slices bread, buttered
1 cup diced store cheese (¼ pound)
2 cups milk
2 eggs
1 teaspoon salt

Cube bread and place in buttered baking dish. Sprinkle cheese over bread. Beat eggs, milk and salt together and pour over bread and cheese. Bake about 1 hour in 350 oven. Will serve 4.

Cheese and Cornmeal Slices

2 cups boiling water
1 cup yellow cornmeal
1 teaspoon salt
1 cup milk
2 cups store cheese, cubed small (½ pound)
flour for dredging
fat for frying

Place boiling water in top of double boiler, add salt. Mix cornmeal with 1 cup milk, stirring until smooth. Add to boiling water, stirring constantly. Let boil for 5 minutes over direct heat. Return over hot water, cover and let steam for about 3 hours, stirring occasionally. Remove from heat, stir in cubed cheese and turn into a standard-size bread tin which has been dipped in cold water. When cold, turn loaf out and slice in ¾-inch slices, dip in flour and fry in

melted fat in a skillet. Brown well on one side,
turn over and brown on other side. These slices
are delicious served with fried ham or bacon.
Serves 5.

Fried Cheesecakes

    1 cup store cheese, grated (¼ pound)
    ½ teaspoon grated lemon rind
    pinch of pepper
    ⅔ cup sour cream
    3 egg yolks, beaten
    2½ tablespoons flour

Combine cheese, flour and seasonings. Add sour
cream and beaten egg yolks. Drop batter in small
spoonfuls onto hot greased griddle. When air
bubbles appear on upper side of cakes, turn carefully and brown on other side. These feathery
little cakes crumple easily and need gentle handling. Serve hot from the griddle as they are
fried. These cakes are especially good with
fried ham. Serves 6 generously.

Cottage Cheese Pancakes

    1 cup cottage cheese
    1 tablespoon melted butter
    1 tablespoon flour
    2 eggs, beaten
    pinch of salt

Put cottage cheese through a sieve and mix with
other ingredients. Beat well. Drop onto hot griddle in quite small cakes and fry until brown on
both sides.

These delicate little cakes break easily, and care should be taken in turning them. They are especially good when spread with a little strawberry jam or just dusted with sugar.

Quick Cheese Sauce

½ pound store cheese, diced very small
1 cup evaporated milk

Scald milk over hot water. Add the cheese and continue cooking until cheese is melted, or about 5 minutes. Stir constantly while cooking to keep sauce smooth and well blended.

Smooth Cheese Sauce

2 tablespoons butter, melted
2 tablespoons flour
1 cup milk
½ teaspoon salt
pinch of pepper
1 egg yolk, beaten
1 cup grated store cheese (¼ pound)

Stir flour into melted butter, add salt, then add the milk slowly, stirring continuously. Add pepper and cook about 4 minutes over very low heat, stirring all the while to prevent lumping. Add cheese and keep hot over boiling water until cheese is melted and has blended with sauce. Just before serving, stir sauce into the beaten egg yolk and return to heat. Stir 1 minute, then serve.

CHAPTER THREE

Meats

THE OLD HANDWRITTEN cookbooks contain virtually no recipes involving steaks and chops. The valued rules were those that used cuts demanding longer and more careful cooking and seasoning, and every housewife treasured receipts for stews and what are now known as "variety meats."

Since fresh pork and beef could be enjoyed only during Winter and early Spring when extreme cold preserved the meat, many recipes were concerned with ways to use sausage, or the ham and bacon which lasted almost year round. And of course there was always salt pork, for the stoneware crock in the cellar was never quite empty of the creamy white slabs of meat laid down in icy brine.

The housewife considered salt pork indispensable, not only when pan-fried to a crisp golden crunchiness and served with boiled potatoes and milk gravy made right in the skillet, but also as a means of flavoring all sorts of dishes. Old-time hill farmers didn't think a boiled dinner worthy of the name unless there was a generous square of salt pork cooked right along with the corned beef and cabbage. Nor would they have dreamed of dandelion greens without a good-sized piece of salt pork boiled in the same pot, with potatoes added during the last part of the cooking. Small wonder that Yankees love the flavors of greens, pork and potatoes subtly blended into a delicious whole!

New England Boiled Dinner

4 pounds corned beef
1 pound salt pork, unsliced
1 large cabbage, quartered
10 large whole carrots, peeled
1 large turnip, peeled and cut large
8 large potatoes, peeled
8 parsnips, peeled
12 small beets, unpeeled

Simmer corned beef and salt pork in unsalted water to cover for about 1 hour. Add turnip, carrots and parsnips. Cook 1 more hour, then add potatoes and cabbage. Meanwhile cook beets in separate kettle in salted water until tender. When corned beef is very tender, remove to platter with salt pork. Drain vegetables and place around meat on platter. Drain beets, immerse in cold water and slip skins off quickly before beets have time to cool. Add to vegetables on platter and serve at once. Serves 6 to 8.

Leftovers may be made into Red Flannel Hash.

Red Flannel Hash

4 cups corned beef (boiled dinner leftover)
4 cups cooked potatoes (from boiled dinner)
4 cooked beets
other leftover vegetables
salt to taste
bacon fat for browning

The amounts given here are intended to show proportions rather than actual measurements, since leftovers seldom come out pat. The rule-of-thumb is to have equal amounts of potatoes and corned beef and enough beets to give the hash a deep red color.

Put corned beef, potatoes, beets and all other leftover vegetables through the meat grinder. Season to taste with salt, and brown in bacon fat in a large spider.

Roast Salt Pork

1½ pounds unsliced salt pork
about 4 cups milk for soaking
¼ teaspoon salt
1 cup dry breadcrumbs
1 teaspoon sage
¼ teaspoon pepper
2 tablespoons hot water
¼ teaspoon pepper (additional)
1 cup milk for baking (additional)
8 small potatoes, peeled

Wash salt pork in clear water, place in kettle and cover with about 4 cups milk. Soak overnight. Drain, discarding milk in which pork was soaked. Score rind with cuts 1 inch deep. Fill cuts with stuffing made by combining breadcrumbs, salt, sage and ¼ teaspoon pepper, then adding the water. Sprinkle ¼ teaspoon pepper over top of meat and place rind down in a baking pan which has a lid. Add 1 cup fresh milk and bake in 375 oven for about 1 hour.

Remove from oven, pour off all liquid except about 2 cups. Place potatoes in ring around meat and return to oven. Cook until potatoes are tender and both meat and potatoes are golden brown. Remove pork and potatoes to serving dish. Skim fat from liquid in pan and thicken with a little flour and water paste stirred until smooth. Serve pork in thin slices, gravy in a sauce boat. Serves 5 to 6.

This is a very old recipe and is included mainly because of its interest, since there are so many calorie-counters today. In my great-grandmother's household this dish was much esteemed, and was often served when other meats were not available.

Pan-Fried Salt Pork

½ pound salt pork, sliced very thin
flour and cornmeal for dredging
2 tablespoons flour for thickening milk
2 cups milk (or sour cream)

Cover pork slices with boiling water and let stand 3 minutes. Do not allow to cook. Remove slices and drain well. In a mixture of equal amounts of flour and cornmeal, dredge slices. Fry in heavy frying pan in their own fat until crisp and golden brown. Remove, drain on brown paper and keep hot. Pour off fat in pan, leaving about 2 tablespoonfuls. Return pan to heat and stir in flour, then add milk, stirring constantly, to make a creamy gravy speckled with tiny crumbs of pork.

Many cooks of long ago substituted sour cream for the milk, and omitted the flour, since the sour cream needs little or no thickening. Serve pork slices and gravy separately, with boiled potatoes. Serves 4 to 5.

For an extra-special touch try Salt Pork in Egg Batter.

Salt Pork in Egg Batter

After frying salt pork slices and draining according to the preceding rule for Pan-Fried Salt Pork, dip each slice in a simple egg batter consisting of: 1 egg beaten well with 1 tablespoon cold water. Pop right back into the hot fat in the spider until slices are golden brown on both sides. Remove, drain and keep hot. Then proceed to make milk gravy or sour-cream gravy as for pan-fried salt pork.

The thick crust of batter covering the crisp, sweet meat makes this a dish well worth the added effort.

Salt Pork and Codfish

½ pound salt codfish, freshened
½ pound fat salt pork, diced small
2 tablespoons flour
2 cups milk

Soak codfish in cold water to freshen, preferably overnight. Drain and pick into shreds. In heavy skillet, fry pork over low heat until crisp and brown. Add shredded codfish, frying all gently. Remove pork and fish from pan and drain on brown paper. Pour away most of fat in frying pan, leaving about 2 tablespoonfuls. Return pan to fire, stir in flour, then add milk, stirring as it cooks to keep gravy smooth. Serve in the old-fashioned way: a serving of the fish and pork on each plate with the gravy spooned over hot boiled or baked potatoes.

This is a very old recipe and is vague as to amounts, leaving them up to the individual cook. It was a welcome change on the farm during the monotony of a long Winter.

Sausage Rolls

½ pound sausage meat
½ rule for Buttermilk Biscuits

Form sausage meat into small rolls, about the size of one's little finger. Fry until well browned, turning frequently. Remove from pan and drain well. Roll out biscuit dough to about ¼ inch thick and cut in small squares about 2½ x 2½. Place a sausage roll on edge of each square and roll. Do not pinch ends of roll together, but press overlapping edge of dough in place firmly. Place on greased pan and bake in 400 oven for about 15 minutes, or until crisp and brown. These crusty little brown rolls can be eaten with the fingers and are a delicious accompaniment to scrambled eggs.

Sausage Scramble

1 pound sausage meat
1 large onion, peeled and diced
4 cold boiled medium potatoes, diced
½ teaspoon salt
pinch of pepper
about ½ cup cream

Crumble sausage in frying pan and fry lightly. Pour off most of the hot fat, add diced onion and simmer over low heat for 5 minutes. Add diced potatoes and seasoning, pour cream over all and continue cooking over low heat until cream is almost all absorbed and the potatoes are brown—the whole resembling an omelet. The amounts of potato and cream will vary with the individual cook, but roughly each cup of diced potato requires around ¼ cup cream. Serves 5 to 6.

Ham Shortcakes with Egg Sauce

    1 cup cooked ground ham
    1 rule for Buttermilk Biscuits

Blend ham into biscuit dough just before adding liquid. Roll out on floured board to about 1 inch thick. Bake on greased pan in 450 oven for 12 minutes or until brown. Serve hot with Egg Sauce.

EGG SAUCE:

    3 hard-boiled eggs, peeled and chopped
    2 cups milk
    4 tablespoons butter
    4 tablespoons flour
    ¾ teaspoon salt
    pinch of pepper

Melt butter, add flour and stir until smooth. Add milk, stirring constantly, and cook over low heat until thickened, about 4 to 5 minutes, continuing to stir so sauce will not lump. Add

seasonings and egg. Remove from heat and serve
at once.

Ham Turnovers

> 1½ cups flour
> ½ cup lard
> 1 teaspoon any baking powder
> ½ teaspoon salt
> cold water

Make this extra-rich biscuit dough by sifting
flour, salt and baking powder together, cutting
in the lard and adding enough cold water to
make the dough stick together. Roll out on
floured board to about ¼ inch thick and cut
in squares 3 x 3 inches. Put a heaping teaspoonful of filling in the center of each square, fold
into a triangle and pinch edges together. Bake
in 400 oven for about 15 minutes. Serve hot.
Serves 5 to 6.

HAM FILLING:

> 2 tablespoons butter
> 2 tablespoons flour
> 1 cup hot milk
> 2 cups ground cooked ham
> 1 small onion, peeled and ground
> pinch of pepper

Make a white sauce by melting butter, stirring
in flour until smooth, then adding milk, stirring
constantly as it thickens. Add ham, onion and
seasonings.

Baked Ham and Corn

1 cup cooked ham, chopped fine
2½ cups fresh corn, cut from cob
1 small green pepper, minced
1 small onion, peeled and chopped fine
2 tablespoons butter
1 cup cream
½ teaspoon salt
pinch of pepper

Simmer green pepper and onion in butter until tender. Add to ham, corn and seasonings. Add cream. Blend well and pour into greased baking dish. Bake uncovered in 400 oven for about 20 minutes. Serves 4.

Stuffed Ham Roll

1 slice ham, 1 inch thick
1 tablespoon minced onion
4 tablespoons butter
4 cups soft breadcrumbs
½ teaspoon salt
1 teaspoon ground sage
1 cup hot water

Sauté onion in the butter until golden brown. Add crumbs and seasonings. Stir until crumbs are well coated with the melted butter. Spread crumb mixture on the ham slice, roll·it lengthwise and tie with string. Place in baking dish which has a lid. Add the water and cover. Bake in 350 oven until ham is tender, about 1½ hours. Serves 5 to 6.

Pot Roast with Prunes

4-pound pot roast
flour for dredging
3 tablespoons fat for browning
3 medium onions, peeled and sliced
½ pound uncooked prunes
1 teaspoon salt
⅛ teaspoon pepper
1½ cups water
¼ cup vinegar
4 whole cloves

Soak prunes overnight. Dredge meat in flour and brown on all sides in fat melted in frying pan. Remove meat to heavy baking dish which has a close-fitting lid. Cook onion slices in the hot fat in frying pan until golden brown and add to meat, together with every bit of fat in pan. Sprinkle with salt and pepper, and arrange prunes around meat. Add water, vinegar and cloves. Cover tightly and bake in 325 oven until tender, about 3½ hours. Serves 6 to 8.

Oven Stew

3 to 4 pounds beef shank
2 medium carrots, peeled and diced
1 very small turnip, peeled and diced
2 medium onions, peeled and diced
3 medium potatoes, peeled and cubed
1½ teaspoons salt
¼ teaspoon pepper
¼ cup catsup
3 cups hot water
flour for dredging

Cut meat from bone and cube. Crack bone and scrape out marrow. Melt marrow in frying pan. Dredge meat in flour and brown in melted marrow. Arrange meat in heavy baking dish which has a close-fitting lid and add turnip, carrots and onions. Add catsup, salt and pepper and about 3 cups hot water. Cover tightly and bake in 300 oven for 2½ hours. Add potatoes and continue cooking until meat is very tender, about 45 minutes more. Serves 8.

This is a good recipe to use when the oven is being used for other baking, because the pot may be tucked in the very back and requires little attention. This oven stew is more flavorful and quite different from an ordinary beef stew made on the top of the stove.

Beef Stew with Dumplings

2 pounds stewing beef
boiling water
3 tablespoons any fat
flour for dredging
2 large onions, peeled and quartered
2 teaspoons salt
¼ teaspoon pepper
1 crumbled bay leaf
4 cups canned tomatoes, undrained
1 small turnip, peeled and cubed
6 carrots, peeled and quartered
4 medium potatoes, peeled and quartered

Cut beef into 1-inch cubes, dredge in flour and brown in the fat melted in bottom of heavy kettle which has close-fitting lid. Cover meat with boiling water, add onions, salt, pepper and bay leaf. Add tomatoes, cover kettle and simmer all slowly for 1 hour and 30 minutes, when meat should be about half done. Add turnip and carrots, cover and continue cooking for about 45 minutes longer. Then add potatoes, cover and continue cooking for about 15 minutes. Meanwhile mix Plain Dumplings, drop by the teaspoonful on top of boiling stew, cook 15 minutes more.

PLAIN DUMPLINGS:

2 cups flour
4 teaspoons baking powder
1 teaspoon salt
2 teaspoons lard
1 cup milk

Sift dry ingredients together, cut in lard and add milk to make soft dough. Drop from teaspoon on top of boiling stew, spacing dumplings so they do not touch each other. Cover tightly and cook 15 minutes. Do not lift the cover while dumplings are cooking, or they will be soggy.

Short Ribs of Beef

3 pounds short ribs of beef
2 medium onions, peeled and quartered
2 cups canned tomatoes, undrained
1 teaspoon paprika
1½ teaspoons salt
¼ teaspoon pepper
flour for dredging
2 tablespoons fat for browning

Cut ribs into serving pieces. Dredge with flour and brown in hot fat in frying pan. Remove and place in heavy baking dish which has a close-fitting lid. Add onions, tomatoes and seasonings. Cover tightly and bake in 325 oven for about 3 hours, or until meat is very tender. Serves 6.

Spicy Meat Loaf

1½ pounds ground beef
½ pound sausage meat
1 medium onion, ground fine
1 egg, beaten
½ cup milk
1 cup soft breadcrumbs

> 1 teaspoon salt
>
> ½ teaspoon ground nutmeg
>
> ½ teaspoon ground allspice
>
> ⅛ teaspoon ground ginger
>
> ¼ teaspoon pepper

Mix meats, onion, egg and milk. Mix seasonings with breadcrumbs, add to meat mixture. Press down well in greased standard-size bread tin. Bake in 350 oven for about 1 hour and 15 minutes. Basting is usually not necessary since meat is quite juicy. Serves 6 to 8.

When cold, slices of this spicy meat loaf make superb sandwiches.

Beef and Tomato Bake

> 1½ pounds ground beef
>
> 2 teaspoons salt
>
> 1 teaspoon pepper
>
> 3 tablespoons any fat
>
> 2 medium onions, peeled and sliced
>
> 6 medium potatoes, peeled and sliced
>
> 4 cups canned tomatoes, undrained

Heat fat in frying pan. Mix beef with pepper and 1 teaspoon of the salt, shape into 6 to 8 cakes and brown in hot fat. Remove cakes and place in baking dish which has a lid, pouring over them all the fat remaining in frying pan. Make a layer of the sliced potatoes and onions over top of meat. Add remaining 1 teaspoon of salt to the tomatoes and pour over all. Cover and bake in 350 oven for about 1½ hours. Uncover the last 30 minutes of baking. Serves 6 to 8.

Meatballs in Gravy

1 pound ground beef
½ pound ground pork
½ cup dry breadcrumbs
1 medium potato, cooked and mashed
1 onion, peeled and ground fine
1 teaspoon ground ginger
1 teaspoon salt
⅛ teaspoon pepper
3 tablespoons fat for browning
2 cups beef broth
1 tablespoon flour
½ cup hot tomato juice (optional)

Mix all ingredients, except fat, liquids and flour, as for meat loaf. Form into small balls and brown in heavy frying pan which has a lid. Remove balls, reduce heat and add broth to frying pan. Thicken with the flour, which has been mixed to a smooth paste with a little cold water, to make a thin gravy. Put meatballs back in the gravy, cover and simmer about 1 hour. Hot tomato juice may be added to the gravy for flavor or consistency, if desired. These meatballs are very good warmed up the second day. Serve with mashed potatoes. Serves 6 to 8.

Meat Soufflé

3 tablespoons butter
2 tablespoons flour
2 cups milk
½ cup dry breadcrumbs
1 small onion, peeled and ground fine
2 cups leftover meat, trimmed and ground
2 eggs
salt and pepper to taste

Make a thin white sauce by adding the flour to the butter melted over low heat, then adding the milk, stirring constantly. When the sauce is smooth and creamy, add breadcrumbs (which will thicken it more) and the ground onion. Add meat, then salt and pepper to taste. Remove from heat. Separate eggs, add slightly beaten yolks to the meat mixture. Beat whites stiff and fold into meat mixture. Pour into deep baking dish which has been greased, and bake in 350 oven for 1 hour. Serves 6.

Any kind of cold cooked meat can be used for this soufflé.

Meat and Mashed Potato Pie

3 cups seasoned mashed potatoes
2 cups ground cooked meat
2¼ cups leftover gravy
½ teaspoon salt
pinch of pepper
1 tablespoon butter, melted
pinch of paprika

Spread a layer of mashed potatoes in bottom of

deep, greased pie plate, using ½ the potato. Add ¼ cup gravy to the ground meat and season with the salt and pepper. Spread meat mixture on layer of potato in baking dish, then add remaining potato in a smooth top layer. Brush top with melted butter and sprinkle paprika over. Bake in 375 oven until browned, about 20 minutes. Serve with the remaining 2 cups gravy, heated very hot, to spoon over each serving. Serves 6.

Any kind of cooked meat or chicken may be used for this dish. If you have no gravy left over to use, try one of the canned or packaged gravies available at any grocery store. If you have a small amount of gravy, try stretching it with a medium white sauce.

Meat and Vegetable Hash

    1 small onion, peeled and diced
    ½ medium green pepper, diced
    1 tablespoon butter
    2 medium tomatoes, peeled and chopped
    2 tablespoons chopped celery
    2 tablespoons chopped parsley
    1 cup water
    2 cups diced cooked beef or pork
    2 tablespoons dry breadcrumbs for thickening
    salt and pepper to taste

Cook onion and green pepper in butter over low heat until tender. Add tomatoes, celery, parsley and water, cook 10 minutes. Add meat and simmer until all is very hot. Stir in breadcrumbs to thicken slightly, and serve at once. This dish is a good way to use leftover meat, and it is especially good served with hot Custard Johnnycake. Serves 4 to 5.

Veal Baked in Sour Cream

2 pounds veal steak
3 tablespoons fat, melted
2 tablespoons flour
1 cup sour cream
1 tablespoon minced onion
½ pound small mushrooms, sliced
2 tablespoons butter for sauteing
1 teaspoon salt

Cut veal into cubes and brown in fat in frying pan. Remove meat to baking dish which has a lid, and stir flour into fat remaining in the spider. When smooth, add sour cream, stirring until thick. Meanwhile simmer mushrooms and minced onion in the butter for 5 minutes. Add to sauce with the salt. Pour sauce over veal, cover and bake in 325 oven for about 1 hour, or until veal is tender. Serves 6.

This veal is delicious, particularly when served with Steamed Rice. (Follow rule under

Vegetables but use 2 cups uncooked rice with 4 cups water and the salt, to serve 6 generously with some to spare.)

Baked Veal Loaf

3 pounds lean veal, ground
½ pound salt pork, ground
6 Common crackers (old-style round ones)
¼ cup milk
1 egg, beaten
2 teaspoons salt
½ teaspoon pepper
1 teaspoon onion juice
2 tablespoons lemon juice
hot water for basting

Crush crackers to make coarse crumbs, mix with veal and pork. Add milk and egg. Add salt, pepper, onion and lemon juices, mixing well. Pack firmly into a large greased loaf pan, about 5 x 12 x 3, and bake in a 300 oven for 2 hours. Baste frequently with a mixture of meat drippings (removed by tilting the pan) and an equal amount of hot water. Prick top of loaf with fork so basting mixture can soak into the meat. This loaf will serve 6 to 8.

Veal Custard

3 cups cooked veal, ground
1 cup broth or milk
2 tablespoons butter
2 eggs
2 tablespoons flour
salt and pepper to taste
1 tablespoon lemon juice

Melt butter, stir in flour and add broth or milk. Cook over hot water until smooth and thick, stirring constantly. Beat eggs well and add to hot sauce slowly, stirring constantly. Add ground veal, lemon juice, then salt and pepper to taste. Pour into greased custard cups and set in pan of warm water. Bake in 350 oven for about 30 minutes. Serve with reheated leftover gravy or with a medium white sauce. Serves 5 to 6.

Baked Spareribs with Apples

        2 strips spareribs
        5 tart apples, peeled and diced
        2 medium carrots, peeled and diced
        2 medium onions, peeled and diced
        1 teaspoon salt
        ¼ teaspoon pepper
        ¼ teaspoon cinnamon
        1 cup water

Put carrots and onions in bottom of heavy baking pan which has a cover. Place one strip of spareribs on top of onions and carrots and sprinkle with ½ of the salt and pepper. Spread diced apples over meat and sprinkle with cinnamon. Lay remaining strip of spareribs on top of apples and hold in place with skewers thrust down through bottom layer of spareribs. Sprinkle top strip with remaining salt and pepper. Add water to pan and cover. Bake in 325 oven for about 1 hour. Uncover and continue baking for about 30 minutes longer, or until meat is tender.

Number served depends upon size of the strips, but the usual allowance is 1 pound of ribs per person.

Cheshire Pork Pie

1 batch Pie Pastry for 2 Crusts
2 pounds lean pork
4 medium apples
2 tablespoons white sugar
1 teaspoon salt
⅛ teaspoon pepper
¼ teaspoon ground sage
1 cup sweet cider
1 tablespoon butter
1 beaten egg

Cut pork in strips 1 x 2 inches. Peel and slice apples. Line a deep pie plate with pie dough rolled about ⅛ inch thick. Put in a layer of pork and sprinkle with a little of the salt, pepper and sage. Next, add a layer of the apple slices with some of the sugar sprinkled over them. Continue making alternate layers of pork and apples until all are used. Add sweet cider and dot top layer with the butter.

Cover with the top crust, in which several slits have been made. Brush crust with beaten egg and bake in 350 oven for about 1 hour and 30 minutes. Serves 6.

Pork Chops Baked with Split Peas

4 meaty pork chops
2 cups dried split peas
½ teaspoon salt
⅛ teaspoon pepper
1 tablespoon fat for browning
1 medium onion, chopped
2 tablespoons honey
1 teaspoon salt (additional)
pinch of pepper (additional)

Soak peas for about 4 hours in water barely covering, then boil for 20 minutes in the same water. Drain and reserve water. Rub chops with the ½ teaspoon of salt and ⅛ teaspoon pepper, and brown in the fat melted in frying pan.

In the bottom of a deep baking dish which has a lid, place a layer of ½ the split peas. Lay chops on the peas, sprinkle with the chopped onion, then add a layer of the rest of the peas. Mix honey with 1 cup of the water in which peas were cooked, add the 1 teaspoon of salt and pinch of pepper. Pour liquid over chops and peas. Cover and bake in 350 oven until all is tender, about 1 hour and 30 minutes. More water should be added if mixture appears dry during baking. Will serve 4.

A simple syrup made from boiling 2 parts sugar to 1 part water may be used instead of honey.

Old-Fashioned Head Cheese

1 hog's head, well trimmed and quartered
salt
pepper

Wash quarters well and put in heavy kettle, cover with unsalted water and simmer until meat falls from bones, about 3 hours. Remove from fire and cool until meat can be handled, but do not let it get so cold that the fat congeals. Drain away liquid and pick bones, gristle and fat from meat.

Place meat in wooden chopping bowl and chop it very fine. Season to taste with salt and pepper. Pack meat mixture in several standard-size bread tins to about ¾ full. Nest one pan on top of another, with waxed paper between each pan, and place a weight on the top pan to press whole properly. Set in cool place overnight. In the morning, slide each loaf from its pan and wrap well in waxed paper. Refrigerate until used.

This head cheese is nothing like the commercial variety and nowadays can be had only from a farmer's wife who still makes it. It's wonderfully good, especially in a sandwich.

Baked Lamb Loaf

3 pounds lean raw lamb, ground
½ pound sausage meat
½ cup dry breadcrumbs
1 egg, beaten
1 tablespoon butter
1 tablespoon flour
½ cup milk
¾ teaspoon salt
¼ teaspoon pepper
½ cup cream for gravy

Mix lamb, sausage, breadcrumbs and egg. Make white sauce by adding flour to melted butter in a small pan, then adding the milk and stirring until it thickens over low heat. Add salt and pepper to sauce, then blend sauce into meat mixture. Pack firmly into a greased large loaf pan, about 5 x 12 x 3, or form into a long loaf on a flat baking pan.

Bake in 325 oven for 1 hour and 30 minutes. Baste from time to time by spooning pan juices over the meat. Remove loaf from pan to serving dish and add ½ cup cream to pan juices. Thicken with a thin paste of flour and water stirred until smooth, cooking for 3 minutes. Serve in a sauce boat. Serves 6 to 8.

Lamb with Green Beans

3 pounds lamb breast, lean
4 cups fresh green beans, cut up
6 small onions, peeled
3 tablespoons any fat
3 cups water
4 tablespoons vinegar
1½ teaspoons salt
⅛ teaspoon pepper
flour for thickening

Cut meat into cubes and brown in melted fat in frying pan. Turn all, including any fat in pan, into a baking dish which has a lid. Place vegetables on top of lamb. Add salt, pepper, water and vinegar. Cover and bake in a 350 oven until meat and vegetables are tender, about 1½ to 2 hours. Shortly before serving, thicken gravy by adding a thin paste of flour and water to ½ cup of the hot liquid, then returning diluted flour paste to the meat and vegetables, blending well. Cook 10 minutes longer. Serves 6.

Lamb Meatballs with Rice

1½ pounds lamb shoulder, lean
6 medium carrots, peeled
1 medium onion, peeled
1 egg, beaten
1 teaspoon salt
⅛ teaspoon pepper
flour for dredging
4 tablespoons fat
½ cup hot water
3 tablespoons flour
1½ cups unsalted broth or water
additional salt to taste
4 cups hot Steamed Rice for serving

Put lamb, carrots and onion through food grinder. Add salt, pepper and egg to meat mixture. Mix well, shape into small balls and dredge in a little flour. Melt fat in frying pan and brown meatballs on all sides. When brown, add ½ cup hot water and cover the pan. Reduce heat and cook slowly for about 10 minutes. Remove meatballs and keep hot. Add 3 tablespoons flour to fat and liquid in frying pan and stir until smooth. Add broth or water. Cook slowly until gravy thickens. Taste and add more salt if desired. Pour gravy over meatballs and serve with hot Steamed Rice. Will serve 5 to 6.

Bouillon cubes dissolved in hot water make a satisfactory broth for this recipe, but no additional salt will be needed if they are used.

Baked Liver

2 pounds beef or pork liver, unsliced
1 teaspoon salt
¼ pound salt pork
1 large onion, peeled and quartered
½ teaspoon sage
½ teaspoon pepper
½ cup water, if needed

Wipe liver but do not scald. With sharp knife, make cuts 1 inch long here and there over surface of liver, and place it in a baking dish which has a lid. Sprinkle with 1 teaspoon salt. Put salt pork and onion through food grinder. Mix with sage and pepper and spread over top of liver. Cover and bake in 400 oven for about 45 minutes. Uncover and bake 20 minutes longer, adding water if dish becomes too dry during baking. The flavors of the salt pork and onion combine very happily with that of the liver. Serves 6.

Batter-Fried Liver

1½ pounds beef liver, sliced fairly thin
1 cup flour
1 teaspoon salt
1 cup milk
2 eggs, beaten
flour for dredging
fat for deep frying

Prepare batter by sifting flour and salt together, adding beaten eggs and milk, blending until smooth. Heat fat slowly in deep, heavy kettle. While it is heating, scald liver by dipping briefly in boiling water, and then drain. Wipe each slice dry and dredge by rolling in flour. For frying, the deep fat should register 370 degrees on a thermometer. If you have no thermometer, drop a 1-inch bread cube in the fat; if bread browns in 1 minute, the fat is the right temperature. Dip each scalded and dredged slice of liver in the batter and place in the hot fat. Liver will rise to the surface when done.

Do not crowd kettle. As each slice is done, remove, drain and keep hot until all liver is fried. Batter-fried liver is a little more trouble than pan-fried, but it is well worth it. Serves 5.

SUBSTITUTIONS:

Pork liver may be used instead of beef.

An equal amount of oil may be used instead of fat.

The amount of fat depends upon the size of your kettle, also upon the amount of liver to be fried. In general, fat for deep frying should be kept to about 2 inches from the top of the kettle.

Cold Boiled Beef Tongue

    1 fresh beef tongue
    2 tablespoons vinegar
    1 tablespoon salt
    4 whole cloves
    3 bay leaves

Wash tongue thoroughly and place in kettle which has a tight-fitting lid. Add water to cover, then add vinegar, salt and spices. Simmer covered until tender, about 3 to 4 hours. Take out tongue and remove skin, fat and gristle. Return to kettle, remove from fire and let cool in the liquid. Drain and chill in refrigerator before slicing.

Tongue cooked this way is excellent for sandwiches, also to serve with potato salad.

Baked Stuffed Heart

    1 large beef heart
    8 cups cold water
    1 cup vinegar
    1 teaspoon salt
    2 cups Sausage Stuffing
    ½ cup water

Soak heart for 1 hour or longer in the cold water, to which the vingear has been added. Drain and cut away fat and tubes. If the heart is large, parboil for 1 hour in fresh water to which the 1 teaspoon of salt has been added. Remove and drain well. Stuff heart with Sausage Stuffing and sew together at top. Place in heavy baking pan which has a lid, add ½ cup fresh water. Cover and bake in 350 oven until heart is tender, about 2 to 3 hours. Serves 6.

Two veal or pork hearts may be used for the same yield. If the smaller hearts are used, parboiling may be omitted and the salt added to the ½ cup of water in pan for baking.

Roast Venison

    5-pound venison roast, from haunch
    ¼ pound salt pork, cut in strips

1 teaspoon salt
⅛ teaspoon pepper
8 cups buttermilk
4 medium onions, peeled and chopped
3 bay leaves

Add bay leaves and onions with the salt to buttermilk to make marinade. Soak venison in marinade for 48 hours, turning each night and morning. Discard marinade and lard venison well with the strips of salt pork tucked into deep slits cut in the meat. Place in roasting pan and roast uncovered in 350 oven until tender, allowing 20 minutes to the pound.

This recipe will turn out venison with no wild taste and will compare favorably with a roast of beef.

Baked Coon

1 coon, dressed and trimmed (around 5 to 6 pounds)
1 tablespoon salt
¼ pound salt pork, sliced thin
1 teaspoon salt (additional)
¼ teaspoon pepper
1 batch Breadcrumb Sausage Stuffing (optional)

Remove all fat possible from dressed coon. Remove the four scent glands, two of which are found deep in the pit under each foreleg and two below the tail. Care should be taken not to cut into glands. For ease in handling, the coon should be quartered, then placed in large kettle and covered with cold water to which the tablespoon of salt has been added. Soak for 24 hours. Drain, cover with fresh, unsalted water and parboil until meat just begins to be tender, about 1 hour. Drain and place in a large fairly shallow baking pan, season with 1 teaspoon salt and ¼ teaspoon pepper. Spoon stuffing around and under the meat, if desired. Lay slices of salt pork across top of meat. Bake uncovered in 375 oven until meat is brown and tender, around 2 hours.

Some rules do not mention the scent glands, but an old man who had hunted the hills of Vermont for seventy years swore they were there and must be removed if I wanted good sweet meat. I wasn't sure just what they looked like, so to be on the safe side I cut a triangle of meat from each area in question and trusted to luck. It worked fine.

There is no better eating than a young coon properly baked. The meat tastes like the most delicate roast pork.

Baked Rabbit

1 rabbit, cleaned and cut up (2 to 3 pounds)
⅓ cup flour
1 teaspoon salt
1 teaspoon sage
3 tablespoons fat, melted
4 cups milk
4 tablespoons butter, melted
4 tablespoons flour (additional)
1 teaspoon salt (additional)
pinch of pepper
3 strips of bacon

Cut rabbit into serving pieces. Mix flour with
sage and 1 teaspoon salt. Dredge meat thoroughly in flour mixture, then brown on all sides
in melted fat. Place meat in baking dish which
has a lid. Lay bacon over the meat. Make white
sauce by blending the 4 tablespoons flour into
the melted butter, then stirring in the 4 cups
milk and cooking over low heat until thickened,
stirring constantly. Add 1 teaspoon of salt and a
pinch of pepper to sauce, then pour over meat.
Cover and bake in 350 oven until meat is tender,
about 2 hours. This will serve 6 to 7.

Either wild or domestic rabbit may be used,
but it may be necessary to cook the wild rabbit
a little longer.

CHAPTER FOUR

Poultry

UNTIL FAIRLY RECENTLY housewives in New England's mountain country had no year-round supply of tender, scientifically raised chickens or broilers, and they depended upon the farm flock to provide for the table. However the result was that they evolved recipes to use fowl and not-so-tender roosters in ways that turned them into miracles of tenderness and goodness. Perhaps it is a trick of memory, but the chickens we find in the supermarkets today seem to me to lack flavor in comparison.

Certainly I've eaten no better fried chicken than made by my mother, who took a year-old bird, steamed or parboiled it until just barely tender, then dredged it in flour and browned it in a heavy frying pan. Her chicken pie, too, was the best I've ever come across, and she scorned the practice of leaving some of the bones in her pie to support the crust. On occasion she stuffed and trussed a fowl past the roasting age, steamed it until nearly tender and then transferred it to a roasting pan, buttering the unbroken skin and lightly dusting it with flour. Baked in a quick oven, it became a crusty, delicious brown, the meat ready to fall from the bones at the first touch of the carving knife.

In my own part of Vermont—the upper Connecticut River valley—turkeys appeared but seldom on day-before-yesterday's menus. Turkeys, which were hard to raise, were considered more trouble than they were worth. So the traditional Thanksgiving dinner that I remember was a long roast of brown and crackling pork at one end of the table, and a mammoth chicken pie awaiting my mother's serving at the other.

Leftover chicken or fowl can be used in a variety of ways, and I found a wide selection of such recipes in almost every old collection. Cooked turkey can, of course, be used in any of the rules calling for chicken.

Chicken and Sour-Milk Dumplings

1 5-to-6-pound fowl
1 large onion, peeled and quartered
2 teaspoons salt
pinch of pepper
8 medium potatoes, peeled
8 medium onions, peeled and parboiled
flour for thickening gravy

Cut up fowl and place in a deep kettle which has a close-fitting lid. Add salt and pepper, the large onion and just enough water barely to cover the chicken. Cover and simmer fowl slowly for about 2 hours. Add potatoes and the 8 onions, which have been parboiled for 20 minutes in salted water and drained. Cover and continue cooking for about 30 minutes more. (The chicken should be tender by now, but if the fowl is an old one it may be necessary to add another 30 minutes of cooking time.) When fowl is fork-tender, mix dumplings and drop in by small spoonfuls on top of simmering chicken and vegetables. Cover tightly while cooking.

Remove chicken, dumplings and vegetables to a deep, hot platter. Skim fat from broth and thicken, using 5 tablespoons flour mixed to a paste with 5 tablespoons cold water, to 5 cups of broth. Simmer 3 minutes, stirring constantly. Arrange chicken in center of platter, surrounded by the vegetables and dumplings. Pour gravy over all and serve at once. Serves 6 to 8.

SOUR-MILK DUMPLINGS:

> 2 cups thick sour milk
> ½ teaspoon baking soda
> 2 eggs, beaten
> 1 scant teaspoon salt
> pinch of pepper
> about 3 to 3½ cups flour

Add soda to the sour milk, then add beaten eggs. Sift salt and pepper with 2½ cups flour and stir into milk mixture. Add enough more sifted flour ¼ cup at a time to make dough stiff enough to drop from spoon. (The amount of flour will vary according to the consistency of milk: very thick sour milk requires less flour than does the thin sour milk. In general, dumpling batter should be a little stiffer than muffin batter, but not quite so stiff as biscuit dough.) Drop dumplings carefully so that they rest on the chicken and vegetables and do not touch each other. Do not lift cover while dumplings are cooking. Cook dumplings 20 minutes if large, about 12 minutes if dumplings are quite small.

Great-Grandmother's Scalloped Chicken

    1 5-to-6-pound fowl
    2½ quarts water
    1 teaspoon salt
    1 large onion, peeled and cut up
    1 cup dry breadcrumbs
    ¼ cup butter, melted

Place cut-up fowl in a kettle which has a lid. Add salt, onion and water. Cover and simmer slowly until meat is ready to leave bones, 2 to 3 hours. The time of cooking will depend upon the age of fowl. Remove kettle from heat and let fowl cool right in the broth. While the bird is cooling, make the Dressing and the Sauce (*see below*). When fowl is cool enough to handle, remove from broth and take meat from bones in fair-sized pieces, saving all skin to use later in the sauce. Skim fat from broth and reserve 1 cup of fat for the sauce.

Grease one large (10 x 15) baking pan or two small ones. Put a layer of the dressing in the bottom of the pan. Cover with ½ the sauce. Then make a layer of the chicken and cover with

rest of the sauce. Stir crumbs in the melted butter until well coated, then sprinkle over top of
chicken mixture in pan. Bake about 30 minutes
in 400 oven until top is nicely browned and all
is bubbling hot.

This will serve a dozen people well. To serve
12 from one old hen—what more could a thrifty
housewife ask? And serve them deliciously, too.

DRESSING:

    giblets from the fowl, cooked
    1½ 1-pound loaves of stale bread
    ½ cup butter
    1 medium onion, peeled and diced
    2 medium stalks celery, trimmed and diced
    1 teaspoon sage
    1 teaspoon salt
    pinch of pepper
    ¾ to 1 cup hot chicken broth

Cook giblets until tender in salted water,
drain and put through food grinder. Cut crusts
from bread and discard. Cut bread into ¾-inch
cubes. Melt butter in a large frying pan. Add

onion and celery and sauté about 5 minutes; then add the bread cubes. Add ground giblets, sage, salt and pepper. Mix well, then moisten with broth. The exact amount of broth is difficult to give, since bread varies in consistency, but do not use too much or the dressing will be heavy. Bake with chicken as directed.

SAUCE:

> cooked skin from chicken, ground
> 1 cup milk
> 4 cups chicken broth
> 1 cup chicken fat
> 1 cup flour
> 1 teaspoon salt
> 4 eggs, slightly beaten

Add 1 cup flour to the 1 cup chicken fat. Heat the 4 cups broth with the milk and stir into the fat and flour mixture. Cook over low heat, stirring constantly, until sauce thickens. Add salt. Remove from fire and stir hot sauce into beaten eggs very slowly so sauce will not curdle. Return to heat and cook 5 minutes, stirring constantly. Remove from stove and add ground chicken skin. Bake with chicken as directed.

Beanpot Baked Chicken

> 5-or-6-pound fowl
> 1 large onion, peeled and quartered
> 2 teaspoons salt
> pinch of pepper
> flour for thickening gravy
> additional salt to taste

You will need for this a large covered beanpot, roomy enough to hold the pieces without crowding. Cut up fowl and fit pieces into pot. Tuck in onion, add the salt and pepper. Add water until it can just be seen, about 1 inch below level of fowl. Cover pot tightly and bake very slowly in 300 oven until tender, about 3½ hours. The chicken should be very tender, the meat almost ready to fall from the bones.

Remove chicken to platter and measure the liquid in the pot. Allowing 1¼ tablespoons flour for each cup of liquid to make a gravy of the proper consistency, mix flour with cold water to make a smooth paste. Add to the gravy, which has been returned to the heat and has come to the boiling point. Cook for 5 minutes, stirring constantly. Serve gravy in sauce boat. Will serve 6 to 8. The gravy will be superb, to my mind much richer than that obtained with plain stewed fowl.

The beanpot may be pushed to the back of the oven and left to simmer there while other baking is being done.

Cream-Baked Chicken

1 5-pound chicken or fowl
flour for dredging
3 tablespoons fat for browning
1 teaspoon salt
pinch of pepper
1 medium onion, peeled and diced
2 cups cream

Cut up chicken and dredge in flour. Brown chicken pieces quickly in melted fat in a skillet, but do not allow the chicken to begin to cook up. Remove pieces to deep baking dish which has a close-fitting lid. Sauté onion in the fat remaining in frying pan until golden, about 5 minutes. Add cream and heat very hot. Sprinkle salt and pepper over chicken and pour the cream sauce over all.

Cover tightly and bake in 300 oven until chicken is tender, about 1 hour if chicken is a young and tender one (an older fowl will take up to 3 hours slow baking, depending upon age). When chicken is tender, remove pieces to serving dish. Sauce may be served spooned over the chicken or separateiy in a sauce boat. If preferred, the sauce may be thickened slightly with flour-and-water paste. Serves 6.

Chicken Turnovers

2 cups flour
1½ teaspoons any baking powder
¾ teaspoon salt
½ cup lard
about ¾ cup water
1 tablespoon butter, softened

Sift flour with salt and baking powder. Rub in the lard and mix with the water into firm dough. Roll out to ¼ inch thick, cut in squares 3½ x 3½ inches, and butter them rather lightly. Mix Chicken Filling (below) and place 2 tablespoons of the filling in the center of each square. Fold over and pinch edges together. Space turnovers on greased cookie sheet and bake in 400 oven until brown, about 15 minutes. Heat gravy remaining from making the filling and spoon over piping-hot turnovers. Serves 4 to 5.

FILLING:

    1 cup cooked chicken, diced
    1 cup leftover stuffing
    2½ cups chicken gravy
    salt and pepper to taste

Add stuffing to diced chicken and mix lightly. Moisten with ½ cup leftover chicken gravy and season to taste with salt and pepper. Place 2 tablespoons filling in center of each square. Heat remaining gravy to spoon over each turnover.

SUBSTITUTIONS:

A medium white sauce may be used instead of the leftover chicken gravy, although it will not give the same delicious flavor as the gravy does.

Chicken Jumble

    3 cups cooked chicken, diced
    2 cups cooked rice
    2 cups medium tomatoes, peeled and cut up
    1 cup chicken broth
    1 large onion, peeled and diced
    3 medium stalks celery, trimmed and diced
    1 medium green pepper, diced
    1 teaspoon salt
    pinch of pepper
    ½ cup dry breadcrumbs
    2 tablespoons butter, melted

Simmer cut-up tomatoes with 1 tablespoon water in a small covered saucepan for 10 minutes. Combine chicken with rice, onion, celery and green pepper. Add tomatoes, broth and seasonings. Stir crumbs in the melted butter until well coated. Sprinkle over top of chicken mixture, which has been poured into greased deep baking dish. Bake in 350 oven for about 1 hour. Serves 7 to 8.

Creamed Chicken in Rice

1 cup milk
2 tablespoons butter, melted
2 tablespoons flour
½ teaspoon salt
pinch of pepper
2 cups cooked chicken, cut up

2 cups cooked rice
1 egg, beaten
5 tablespoons butter, melted
½ teaspoon salt
pinch of pepper
1 teaspoon turmeric
3 tablespoons dry breadcrumbs

Make white sauce by stirring the flour into the 2 tablespoons melted butter, then adding the milk and stirring constantly over low heat until smooth and thick. Season with the ½ teaspoon of salt and pinch of pepper, then add chicken. Remove from heat.

Mix rice with the egg and 4 tablespoons of the melted butter. Add ½ teaspoon salt and pinch of pepper; add turmeric. Press into deep pie plate to form a crust. Pour in the creamed chicken. Mix the dry crumbs with the remaining 1 tablespoon of melted butter, and sprinkle over the chicken. Bake in 350 oven for about 20 minutes or until all is very hot, the top nicely browned. Serves 5 to 6.

Rolled Chicken Pancakes with Sauce

> 2 tablespoons minced onion
> 1 tablespoon butter, melted
> 1 cup chopped cooked chicken
> ½ teaspoon salt
> 2 tablespoons sauce (*see below*)

Sauté onion in the melted butter until golden, about 5 minutes. Add chicken, season with salt and moisten with the 2 tablespoons sauce. Keep hot over hot water until ready to use.

SAUCE:

> 1½ cups unseasoned chicken broth
> ¼ cup thin cream
> 2 tablespoons chicken fat (or melted butter)
> 2 tablespoons flour
> 1 egg, beaten
> salt and pepper to taste
> ¼ cup cream, whipped

Heat broth added to the ¼ cup thin cream. Stir the flour into chicken fat or melted butter, then add broth mixture, stirring over low heat until smooth and thickened. Remove from heat and add very slowly to beaten egg, stirring constantly so sauce will not curdle. Return to stove and cook over low heat for 5 minutes more, continuing to stir. Keep hot over hot water until used, when whipped cream should be added.

PANCAKES:

> 1 cup flour
> pinch of salt
> pinch of nutmeg
> 1 egg, beaten
> 1½ cups milk

Sift flour with salt and nutmeg. Add egg to milk, then blend all well with egg beater. Use ¼ cup batter for each pancake. Drop from cup to hot greased griddle. Brown lightly on one side, turn carefully and brown lightly on other side. Cakes will be very thin and take only about a minute to cook on each side. Do not overcook or they will be hard to roll.

To serve, put 1 tablespoon of the chicken filling on each pancake, spreading lengthwise along center. Roll. Whip the ¼ cup cream and fold into sauce. Serve a generous spoonful across each pancake. Serves 5 to 6.

Old-Fashioned Sausage Stuffing

2½ cups flour

1 teaspoon salt

1 teaspoon baking soda

1½ cups thick sour cream

2½ teaspoons cream of tartar

1 pound sausage meat

2 teaspoons ground sage

2 eggs, beaten

1 teaspoon salt (additional)

pinch of pepper

½ cup hot broth or milk

Sift flour with soda, cream of tartar and 1 teaspoon salt. Mix in the sour cream. Turn out on floured board, divide dough into 3 equal parts. Pat, do not roll, into 3 mounds, about 1 inch thick. Place on greased cookie sheet and bake in 450 oven for about 15 minutes, or until crispy brown.

Cool and crumble into large bowl. Add sausage, eggs, sage, 1 teaspoon salt and the pepper. Add beaten eggs. Moisten with ½ cup hot broth or milk and mix thoroughly. Stuff bird the day before, if possible, keeping in refrigerator until ready to roast. This amount of stuffing will be sufficient for 2 5-pound chickens or 1 16-to-18-pound turkey.

This is one of the best sausage stuffings I know of, because the base of sour-cream biscuits seems to add a flavor that ordinary bread does not give.

Breadcrumb Sausage Stuffing

3 cups stale breadcrumbs
2 teaspoons sage or poultry seasoning
1 teaspoon salt
⅛ teaspoon pepper
½ pound sausage meat
¼ cup melted sausage fat
½ cup hot water

Add seasonings to breadcrumbs. Fry sausage meat gently for about 10 minutes, but do not let it get crisp and brown. Remove meat and drain, reserving ¼ cup of the fat. Add fat to breadcrumbs and seasonings, then add sausage meat. Stir in the hot water. Mix well but do not beat.

Great-Grandmother's Salt Pork Stuffing

½ pound salt pork, ground
5 medium onions, peeled and ground
⅓ cup hot water
1 1-pound loaf bread
¼ teaspoon salt
1 teaspoon pepper

Mix salt pork and onions together and simmer gently in large frying pan until tender, about 15 minutes. Add bread, cut in ½-inch cubes. Add water, salt and pepper. Cook all gently until onions are done and stuffing is blended, stirring occasionally, about 20 minutes. Cool before stuffing bird. This amount of stuffing is right for a 10-to-12-pound turkey. Halve the amounts for a 5-pound chicken.

This may seem like a lot of pepper, but it's necessary to give the proper taste to this extremely old rule for turkey stuffing. I don't know exactly how old it is, but I do know that my great-grandmother brought it with her when she married, and she got it from *her* mother. I've never seen it anywhere in any cookbook.

CHAPTER FIVE

Vegetables

THE GARDEN provided a major part of meals in Summer and determined, as well, whether or not the family would have enough to eat during the Winter.

Old-fashioned homemakers were masters at turning the harvest into all sorts of good eating. It was considered a poor year if less than four or five hundred quarts of vegetables and fruit were not put away down cellar. This was food that cost nothing—unless one counts the backbreaking labor of growing, gathering and canning. But when the garden was knee-deep in snow and the north wind whistled, these jars of vegetables and preserves came into their own.

Dandelion Greens and Potatoes with Cornmeal Dumplings

3 pounds dandelion greens
1 teaspoon salt
¼ pound salt pork
6 medium potatoes

Pick over and wash dandelions thoroughly in several waters. Place in kettle which has a close-fitting lid, cover with unsalted boiling water. Set over direct heat and boil rapidly for about 10 minutes to remove any lingering traces of sand. Drain, then half-cover with fresh boiling water, adding the 1 teaspoon salt. Slice salt pork in thin slices down to the rind, so that pork is still held in one piece, and add, tucking down among the greens. Cover and simmer for about 1 hour. Add potatoes, cover and cook for about 30 minutes more. Make Cornmeal Dumplings (*below*) and drop by small spoonfuls on top of boiling greens and potatoes. Don't crowd dumplings. Cover tightly and cook about 15 minutes.

Remove greens, potatoes and dumplings to separate serving dishes or arrange on one large platter. Finish cutting salt pork through the rind and lay the slices over the greens as a garnish. Serves 6.

The first boiling to remove sand also tends to take away some of the bitter tang of the dandelions, to which some people object. Beet greens or Swiss chard may be used instead of dandelions, omitting the first boiling.

CORNMEAL DUMPLINGS:

    1 cup flour
    1¼ teaspoons salt
    2 teaspoons any baking powder
    1 cup cornmeal
    1 egg, beaten
    about ¾ cup milk

Sift flour with salt and baking powder. Add cornmeal. Stir in egg and milk. Batter should be soft. Drop from spoon on top of boiling greens. Cover and cook 15 minutes. Serves 6.

New Potatoes and Cabbage with Cheese

> 1 medium new cabbage, cut rather fine
> same amount new potatoes, peeled and cubed
> 1 cup thin cream
> 1 cup grated store cheese (¼ pound)
> salt and pepper to taste

Cook potatoes and cabbage until tender in just enough salted water to cover. Most of the water will be absorbed in the cooking. While vegetables are cooking, combine the cream with the grated cheese and heat until cheese melts, but do not boil. Pour this sauce over piping hot potatoes and cabbage, and season to taste with salt and pepper. Serve at once. Serves 6 to 8.

Old potatoes and cabbage may be used, but the new vegetables give much the best flavor.

Scalloped Potatoes with Cheese

Scalloped potatoes may be varied by adding grated or finely diced store cheese between the layers of potatoes and onions at a ratio of 1 cup of cheese to 4 large potatoes. Bake as usual. This makes a fine casserole to serve with either hot or cold ham.

Potato Pancakes

2 cups grated raw potatoes
¼ cup milk
1 egg, well beaten
2 tablespoons flour
1 tablespoon grated onion
1 teaspoon salt
pinch of pepper

Add potato to milk and beaten egg. Add rest of ingredients. Mix well and fry in small cakes on a hot greased griddle, slowly turning until brown and crisp. Serve very hot. Will make 12 small cakes.

These potato pancakes are particularly good served with warm applesauce. They are equally good served with a Smooth Cheese Sauce. Be sure that the sauce is very hot as it is spooned over the pancakes, which are piping hot from the griddle.

Fried Potatoes with Salt Pork

4 ¼-inch slices salt pork, diced
1 medium onion, peeled and diced
5 medium potatoes, peeled and sliced
½ teaspoon salt
pinch of pepper

Fry salt pork gently in heavy frying pan for about 10 minutes. Add onion and continue cooking for 5 minutes. Add potatoes, salt and pepper, cover and fry gently until potatoes are tender. Stir and turn contents of pan from time to time to prevent sticking. When turned into serving dish, potatoes should be partly brown, and bits of pork and onion will be scattered throughout. Serves 6.

Warm Potato Salad

8 medium potatoes, peeled
1 teaspoon salt for boiling
4 large strips bacon
1 medium onion, peeled and diced
3 tablespoons sugar
1 tablespoon flour
1 teaspoon salt (additional)
pinch of pepper
¼ cup vinegar
2 tablespoons water

Boil potatoes until just tender in water to cover, adding the 1 teaspoon salt. While potatoes are cooking, dice bacon and fry until crisp and brown. Add onion and fry very gently until tender, about 5 minutes. Mix sugar with flour, more salt and the pepper and add to bacon mixture. Add the water and vinegar. Stir until smooth, and simmer about 3 minutes. Pour over drained hot, sliced potatoes, and mix gently but well. Serve at once. Will serve 8.

Potato Salad

> 6 large potatoes, peeled
> 1 teaspoon salt for boiling
> 1½ tablespoons salad oil
> 1½ tablespoons vinegar
> 1 small onion, peeled and chopped
> 4 hard-boiled eggs, peeled and chopped
> about ¾ cup creamy salad dressing
> salt and pepper to taste

Cook potatoes in water to cover, with the 1 teaspoon of salt. Drain when just tender. Turn into a large bowl and break potatoes apart while still hot, using a fork. Mix the oil and vinegar and sprinkle over potatoes. Cool, then add the onion and the chopped hard-boiled eggs. Add creamy salad dressing. (The commercial dressings are fine. How much to use is difficult to give exactly, since potatoes vary in size and so does the taste of individual cooks. I like a rather moist potato salad.) Season to taste with salt and pepper. Chill before serving. Serves 7 to 10.

This is the rule used by one of the best cooks I've ever known, and she was justly famed for her potato salad for many years. She was un-yielding on several points: (1) potatoes, prefer-ably old ones, must be freshly boiled and should be broken apart while hot; (2) mayonnaise is too bland to spark a good potato salad properly and (3) enough salad dressing should be used to make a moist product. For a variation, she often replaced 2 tablespoons of the salad dressing with an equal amount of sour cream, which changed the flavor subtly and wonderfully.

Baked Soufflé Potato

> 3 cups mashed potatoes (about 6 medium)
> 1 egg, beaten
> ½ cup cream
> 3 tablespoons grated onion
> salt and pepper to taste

Add cream to beaten egg, then beat in mashed potatoes, salt, pepper and onion. Continue beating until light and fluffy, pile into a buttered baking dish and bake in 400 oven until brown, about 15 minutes if mashed potatoes were hot. If cold, leftover mashed potatoes are used, increase baking time to 20 minutes in 375 oven. Serves 6.

Adding 1½ cups ground cooked meat, or flaked canned salmon or even drained whole-kernel corn makes this a fine supper dish.

Potato Patty Shells

> 2 cups hot mashed potatoes (about 4 medium)
> 1 egg, beaten
> 1 tablespoon cream
> 1 teaspoon any baking powder
> 2 tablespoons butter, melted
> ¾ teaspoon salt
> pinch of pepper

Add cream to beaten egg, then add melted butter, salt and pepper. Beat egg mixture into mashed potatoes and continue beating until light and fluffy. Use ⅓ cup of the mixture for each patty shell, forming small round mounds on a greased baking sheet. Make a depression on the top of each mound with the back of a tablespoon. Bake in 400 oven until each patty shell is nicely browned, about 10 minutes. Makes 6 shells.

Serve filled with creamed chicken or fish. If preferred, ½ cup may be used to make each shell, in which case the yield will be 4 large shells.

Vermont Baked Beans

2½ cups dried yellow-eye beans
½ teaspoon baking soda
¾ teaspoon salt
½ teaspoon dry mustard
½ cup maple syrup
½ pound salt pork
hot water

Soak beans overnight in cold water to cover. The next morning, drain and parboil in water to cover, to which the soda has been added. Simmer until the skin of a bean cracks when blown upon: *do not overcook*. Drain again and pour beans into a beanpot. Mix salt, mustard and maple syrup, pour over beans. Score salt pork deeply and lay on top of beans. Add hot water until it can just be seen. Cover and bake very slowly in 275 oven until salt pork is tender and brown, about 4 hours—but 5 or 6 hours would be still better. Replenish water if it cooks away, since beans should not be dry when served. The amount of maple syrup may be a little more or a little less, depending upon how sweet you like your baked beans. Serves 6 to 8.

Maple Candied Sweet Potatoes

6 large sweet potatoes, unpeeled
2/3 cup maple syrup
1 teaspoon salt
2 tablespoons butter
1 cup sweet apple cider
1/3 cup water

Wash potatoes and boil unpeeled until nearly tender. Drain and cool enough to handle. Peel and slice fairly generously, about 1 inch thick, and place in buttered baking dish. Add salt and butter to maple syrup, then add sweet cider and the water. Bring to the boiling point and pour over the sweet potatoes. Bake in 300 oven for about 1 hour. Baste occasionally by spooning syrup in pan over the potatoes. Will serve 6 to 8.

Open Onion Tart

1½ cups flour
2 teaspoons baking powder
½ teaspoon salt
1/3 cup lard
about 2/3 cup milk

Sift flour with baking powder and salt. Cut in

lard and add milk to make a firm, elastic dough. Roll out on floured board to about ⅓ inch thick. Line large (10-inch) pie plate and fill. Bake in 350 oven until filling is set, about 30 minutes. Serves 6.

ONION FILLING:

    2¼ cups chopped onions (about 4 medium)
    2 tablespoons butter, melted
    ¼ teaspoon salt
    pinch of pepper
    ¼ teaspoon nutmeg
    2 eggs, beaten
    1 cup sour cream

Simmer onions in melted butter until very tender but not brown, about 10 minutes. Add salt and pepper and spread on uncooked pastry in pie plate. Mix eggs and nutmeg with sour cream and pour over onions.

Baked Apples and Onions

    12 medium tart apples, peeled and sliced
    3 medium onions, peeled and sliced
    2 tablespoons butter
    1 teaspoon salt
    pinch of pepper
    ½ cup dry breadcrumbs
    1 tablespoon butter (for crumbs)
    ½ cup water

Place about ½ the apples in bottom of a buttered deep baking dish which has a lid. Cover this layer of apples with ½ the onion slices, which have been separated into rings. Dot with 1 tablespoon of the butter and ½ the salt and pepper. Add a layer of the remaining apples, then the remaining onion slices and dot with remaining tablespoon butter and salt and pepper.

Toss crumbs in 1 tablespoon of butter, which has been melted. Sprinkle over top of onions and apples in baking dish. Add ½ cup water. Cover and bake slowly in 350 oven until tender, about 2 hours. A little more hot water may be added if mixture begins to stick on during the baking. Will serve 8.

The amounts of apples and onions may be varied. If you're very fond of onions, use more. An old lady I used to know made this apple-and-onion recipe in her heavy iron spider, simmering the mixture on the back of the stove. Baked or simmered, it's a superb partner to a succulent length of roast pork.

Creamed Carrots and Onions

5 medium carrots, peeled and sliced thin
2 medium onions, peeled and sliced thin
¾ teaspoon salt
¾ cup grated store cheese
3 tablespoons butter
3 tablespoons flour
1½ cups milk
½ teaspoon salt (additional)
pinch of pepper
¼ cup dry breadcrumbs
2 tablespoons butter, melted (for crumbs)

Add carrots to onions and cook until tender in

boiling water to which the ¾ teaspoon of salt
has been added. Drain and place ½ the carrots
and onions in bottom of buttered baking dish.
Add cheese and cover with remaining carrots
and onions.

Make a white sauce by stirring flour into the 3
tablespoons butter, which has been melted,
then adding the milk; cook over low heat, stirring constantly, until smooth and thick. Add
the ½ teaspoon of salt and the pepper. Pour
over the carrots and onions in baking dish. Stir
dry crumbs into melted butter until well coated.
Sprinkle over top of mixture in baking dish
and bake in 375 oven until top is nicely browned
and all is bubbling hot, about 20 minutes.
Serves 6 to 8.

Green Corn Cakes

8 large ears fresh garden corn
2 tablespoons flour
½ teaspoon salt
pinch of pepper
2 egg yolks, beaten
2 egg whites, beaten stiff

Scrape, *don't cut,* the kernels from the ears of
corn. Add flour, salt and pepper. Beat egg yolks
well and add. Fold in stiffly beaten egg whites.
Drop by teaspoons onto hot greased griddle.
When brown on under side, turn and fry about
1 minute more. Serves 6.

These incredibly delicious little cakes deserve
their own niche in some culinary hall of fame.
No one ever believes my description of them

until they've tried this recipe. These are especially good served with fried chicken, and should be served hot from the griddle.

German Beets

4 cups sliced cooked beets
2 medium onions, peeled and sliced
¾ cup sugar
4 tablespoons butter, melted
2 teaspoons cornstarch
⅓ cup vinegar
⅓ cup water
¼ teaspoon salt
pinch of pepper

Simmer onions in melted butter in frying pan until tender but not brown. Stir in sugar, cornstarch, salt and pepper. Stir in water and vinegar. Simmer until thickened, stirring constantly. Add beets. Keep hot over hot water for about 30 minutes to blend flavor of sauce through the beets. Serves 6 to 8.

Summer Squash with Sour Cream

2 medium summer squashes, unpeeled
1 teaspoon salt
1 medium onion, peeled and diced
¼ cup butter
2 cups sour cream
2 tablespoons flour
salt and pepper to taste

Cut squashes into 1-inch cubes and sprinkle with the 1 teaspoon salt. Let stand for about 1 hour, then drain away liquid drawn from squash by the salt. Melt butter in a large frying pan and add diced onions and cubes of squash. Cook very slowly until squash is tender—about 30 minutes—stirring from time to time. Mix sour cream with flour and add to squash, simmering until all is hot, about 5 minutes. Season to taste with salt and pepper. Serves 6.

People who are convinced they don't like summer squash should try this.

Fried Squash Blossoms

    12 squash blossoms
    2 eggs, beaten
    flour for dipping
    ¼ cup bacon fat for frying

Pick the squash blossoms before the sun is hot enough to wilt them. Choose the false blossoms that do not already have small squashes formed. They may be kept fresh in cold water in a cool place until ready to use.

Remove pistils and stamens and dry carefully. Flatten each blossom gently. Dip in the beaten egg, then in flour. Fry in bacon fat, melted and sizzling hot in the spider. Brown on one side, turn carefully and brown on other. Drain on brown paper until all are fried, and serve at once.

Do not fry blossoms until the rest of meal is ready to be served, since they will not stay crisp very long. Allow 3 blossoms per person. A very old recipe, quite unusual and delicious.

SUBSTITUTIONS:

Any fat may be used for frying, but will not be quite so flavorful as that from bacon or sausage.

Savory String Beans

        4 cups cooked string beans
        2 medium onions, peeled and sliced thin
        3 tablespoons butter
        2 cups canned tomatoes, undrained
        1 teaspoon salt
        ¼ teaspoon pepper
        2 whole cloves
        2 teaspoons sugar

Simmer onions in 2 tablespoons of the butter in frying pan until tender but not brown, about 10 minutes. Add tomatoes, salt, pepper, sugar and cloves. Bring to a boil and add string beans. Simmer about 15 minutes. Remove cloves which can easily be seen and taken out with the point of a teaspoon (or cloves could have been tied in small cheesecloth bag.) Add remaining tablespoon of butter and serve at once. Serves 8.

String Beans with Sour-Cream Sauce

        5 cups hot cooked string beans
        1 cup sour cream
        2 tablespoons butter
        1 tablespoon onion juice
        salt and pepper to taste

Drain hot beans. Heat sour cream very hot with

butter and onion juice, but do not boil. Pour over beans, add salt and pepper to taste. Serves 6 to 8.

Steamed Rice

    1 cup rice
    1 teaspoon salt
    2 cups water

Add salt to water in the top of a double boiler and bring to boiling over direct heat. Shake in the cup of rice, stir and boil for 3 minutes, uncovered. Cover and place top of double boiler over lower section, which contains amout 2 cups boiling water. Place over low heat and steam, without lifting cover, until rice is tender, about 30 minutes. Test by rubbing a rice grain between two fingers: if no hardness is felt in the center of the grain, the rice is done, and the water should be absorbed.

This amount of raw rice makes nearly 4 cups cooked, and will serve 4 if used for a main dish, but is sufficient for 6 to 8 if used as a side dish.

Boiled Rice

    1 cup rice
    8 cups boiling water
    1 teaspoon salt

Add salt to boiling water and add rice slowly so water does not stop boiling. Boil uncovered until grains are tender, about 20 minutes. Remove from heat and drain in colander. Pour boiling water briefly over rice to remove starch and to separate the grains of rice. Drain well, return to kettle in which rice was cooked, cover and let dry out on back of the stove (not over heat) for 5 to 10 minutes, or until each grain of rice appears distinct, dry and fluffy. Serves 4 to 8, depending upon method of serving.

Cabbage with Sour-Cream Dressing

1 medium cabbage, shredded
pinch of baking soda
½ cup sour cream
1 tablespoon vinegar
1 tablespoon sugar
salt and pepper to taste

Cook cabbage for about 5 minutes in water to cover, to which the pinch of soda has been added. Drain and cover with freshly boiling water. Cook for 15 minutes more, then drain very well. Pour sour cream over hot cabbage, then add vinegar, sugar, salt and pepper. Mix all thoroughly. Serve at once. Will serve 6 to 8.

Vegetable Oyster Patties

6 large salsify roots (oyster plant)
1 beaten egg
½ teaspoon salt
pinch of pepper
1 tablespoon butter, melted
fat for frying
flour for dusting

Wash and scrape salsify roots. Slice and boil until tender in water to cover, about 30 minutes. Drain and mash well. There should be about 2 cups when mashed. Mix salsify with beaten egg, seasonings and melted butter. Shape into small cakes (about 2 tablespoonsful to 1 cake), dust on each side with flour and fry in a small amount of hot fat in frying pan. Brown on one side, turn and brown on the other. These little cakes are very good and really do taste like oysters. Serves 4.

CHAPTER SIX

Breads, Doughnuts and Pancakes

BAKING DAY was usually Saturday, and it was sometimes very late in the afternoon before the last cake was frosted, the last pie put away. The capacious ovens of those black iron cookstoves were filled with as many loaves of bread as they could accommodate, for it took eight oversized loaves of yeast bread to last the week, even supplemented by biscuits, muffins and johnnycake. A week's supply of doughnuts was fried now, too, and the wooden bucket in the back pantry filled to the brim. The widespread habit of dunking was doubtless encouraged by doughnuts that were five or six days old.

Yeast was hard to come by in the early years, but good bread could be made with milk yeast —"milk emptyings," as my grandmother called this means of leavening. It was a mixture of boiling water, milk, salt, sugar, baking soda and flour, and it rose madly when set in a warm place. It was the basis of very good bread but needed careful attention since, when it's ready, milk yeast won't wait.

Too, there was salt-rising bread, which many people still like for its slightly different and very pleasing taste, especially good when freshly baked. And of course there were all the quick breads that any good hill-country cook could stir up at a moment's notice. Johnnycake was not only a bread but was also often used as the heartier part of a meal—with dried-beef or salt-pork gravy spooned over a hot square; or split hot and buttered with a fried egg and a strip of bacon laid between the halves, or sometimes the yellow cornbread was just crumbled into a bowl of cold milk for Sunday night supper.

And pancakes—which I believe came fully into their own when first served with that unparalleled delicacy from New England's hillsides called maple syrup.

NOTE: More rules for a variety of breads will be found in Chapter Nine, *Maple Sugar and Maple Syrup.*

Plain White Potato Bread

3 medium potatoes, peeled and sliced
3 cups unsalted water
1 yeast cake (or envelope)
2 tablespoons sugar
2 tablespoons shortening
1 tablespoon salt
about 6 cups flour

Boil potatoes in unsalted water until very tender. Do not drain, but mash potatoes right in the liquid. Dissolve shortening, salt and sugar in 2 cups of the mashed potato and liquid. Cool to lukewarm. Cool ¼ cup more of the liquid and dissolve yeast in it. Add softened yeast to lukewarm first mixture. Stir in flour gradually.

Turn onto floured board and knead well, adding a little more flour if needed. Place in a large bowl, cover and let rise in a warm place until doubled in bulk. Turn out on floured board, knead until smooth, divide and place in 2 greased, standard-size bread tins. Cover with a towel and let rise again until doubled. Bake in 350 oven for about 45 minutes.

Potatoes seem to have the wonderful ability to urge yeast into vigorous action, and huge, crusty loaves of snowy bread result. This is my standby rule for all white bread.

White Bread

> 1 cup milk, scalded
> 1 cup boiling water
> 2 tablespoons lard
> 2½ teaspoons salt
> 2 tablespoons sugar
> 1 yeast cake (or envelope)
> ¼ cup lukewarm water
> about 6 cups flour

Add boiling water to hot milk, then add lard, sugar and salt. Cool to lukewarm and add yeast dissolved in the ¼ cup lukewarm water. Stir in about 2 cups of the flour to make a smooth batter. Cover and let rise in a warm place until sponge is light and bubbly, about 1 hour. Add remaining flour, turn out on floured board and knead until dough is smooth and elastic. Return to bowl, cover and let rise again until doubled.

Turn out on floured board, knead down, divide into two halves, and shape each into a loaf. Place in greased standard bread tins, cover with towel and let rise until doubled. Bake in 375 oven for about 50 minutes. Remove from tins, brush tops of loaves with melted butter while still hot. Cool before slicing.

NOTE: Sponge from this rule can be used for making Old-Fashioned Bread Doughnuts.

Salt-Rising Bread

1 cup milk, scalded
⅓ cup white cornmeal
2 teaspoons salt
2 tablespoons sugar
1 cup warm water
2 tablespoons lard
about 5 cups flour

Stir the cornmeal into the hot milk, add 1 teaspoon of the salt and 1 tablespoon of the sugar. Place in a covered container such as a glass jar or pitcher and set in a pan of very warm water to ferment overnight. Batter must not be allowed to cool during this period or fermentation will stop. In the morning, batter should show signs of fermentation: a distinctive but not unpleasant odor, with small gas bubbles heard escaping.

Mix 1 cup warm water with the remaining salt and sugar and the lard. Add to cornmeal mixture, then stir in about 2 cups of the flour. Cover and set again in pan of very warm water and leave until mixture is light and appears full of bubbles. Add rest of flour to make a rather stiff dough. Knead until smooth, shape into 2 loaves and place in greased standard bread tins. Cover with a towel and let rise until doubled. Bake in 350 oven for about 40 minutes.

Salt-rising bread is never quite as light as yeast bread and loaves will not be as large as other kinds. It is a different and most delicious bread and many older people still prefer it to other kinds.

Christmas Bread

2 medium potatoes, peeled and sliced
2 cups unsalted water
2 cups milk, scalded
2 yeast cakes (or envelopes)
9½ cups flour
⅔ cup shortening
2 cups sugar
2 eggs, beaten
3 teaspoons salt
4 cups seeded raisins
½ pound citron, cut fine
2 tablespoons butter, melted
2 teaspoons sugar for topping
¾ teaspoon cinnamon for topping

Boil potatoes in the unsalted water until very tender. Drain, and reserve 1 cup of the water and cool to lukewarm. Mash the potatoes. Dissolve yeast in the reserved cup of lukewarm water. Cool scalded milk to lukewarm and add to yeast mixture. Stir in 1 cup of mashed potatoes and about 3 cups of the flour. Beat well, cover and let rise in a warm place for about 1½ hours.

Cream the shortening with the 2 cups of sugar, beating well. Add beaten eggs and salt. Stir this mixture into the bread sponge and add remainder of the flour. Dough will be soft. Beat all well. Mix in the raisins and the citron. Cover and let rise until doubled. Punch dough down, turn out on floured board and shape into 3 round loaves. Place each loaf in a greased round layer-cake pan (8 x 1½). Brush tops of loaves with the melted butter, and sprinkle with the sugar and cinnamon, which has been mixed together. Cover with a towel and let rise until doubled. Bake in 350 oven for about 1 hour. Finished loaves will be plump and round, like pillows.

This very good and attractive bread makes a welcome gift at Christmas.

Cheese Light Bread

1½ cups grated store cheese
2 tablespoons sugar
1 teaspoon salt
¾ cup boiling water
2 tablespoons shortening
1 yeast cake (or envelope)
¼ cup lukewarm water
1 egg
about 3½ cups sifted flour

Dissolve cheese, sugar, salt and shortening in the boiling water. Cool. Dissolve yeast in the ¼ cup lukewarm water and add to first mixture when all is cooled to lukewarm. Beat in the egg, then add enough sifted flour to make a soft dough. Mix well, turn out on floured board and knead well. Let rise until double in bulk, then knead down again. Shape and place in greased standard size bread tin. Cover with towel and let rise again until double in bulk. Bake in 350 oven for about 50 minutes.

Cinnamon Bread

½ cup cornmeal
2 cups boiling water
1 teaspoon salt
3 tablespoons lard
1 yeast cake (or envelope)
½ cup lukewarm water
½ cup light molasses
5 cups flour
3 tablespoons cinnamon

Stir cornmeal into boiling water and cook for about 5 minutes. Add lard and salt. Cool to lukewarm, then add yeast which has been dissolved in the ½ cup lukewarm water. Add molasses, then stir in 2 cups of the flour to make a sponge. Cover and let rise in a warm place for about 1 hour. Then add remaining 3 cups of flour to make a rather stiff dough. Knead well on floured board, place in a large covered bowl and let rise until doubled.

Turn out on floured board, knead down and divide dough in two equal parts. Roll out each so that the width corresponds to the length of the bread tin you are to use. Thickness of dough will depend upon size of your tin. Sprinkle the halves of dough with the cinnamon and roll each up. Fit into two greased bread tins. Cover with a towel and let rise again. Bake in 350 oven for about 45 minutes.

This bread has a delicious fragrance and is very attractive when sliced.

Squash Rolls

> 1 cup milk, scalded
> ⅓ cup butter
> ⅓ cup sugar
> 1 teaspoon salt
> 1 cup cooked mashed squash
> 1 yeast cake (or envelope)
> ¼ cup lukewarm water
> about 4 cups flour

Combine hot milk with butter, sugar and salt. Cool to lukewarm, then add the squash and yeast, which has been dissolved in the ¼ cup lukewarm water. Stir in sifted flour, using a little more if necessary to make a rather firm dough. Cover and let rise in a warm place until doubled.

Turn out on floured board, knead until smooth, roll to about ⅓ inch thick and cut out with a round biscuit cutter. Place rounds on greased baking pan (8 x 12) and cover with a towel. Let rise again until doubled, then bake in 400 oven for about 20 minutes. Makes 24 to 30 rolls.

Pumpkin may be used satisfactorily instead of squash.

Cornmeal Raised Rolls

    2 cups milk
    ½ cup cornmeal
    ⅓ cup sugar
    ½ cup butter
    1 egg, beaten
    1 teaspoon salt
    1 yeast cake (or envelope)
    ¼ cup lukewarm water
    about 3½ cups flour

Scald milk and add cornmeal, cook for about 5 minutes, stirring constantly. Remove from heat and add sugar and butter. Cool, then add beaten egg, salt and yeast, which has been dissolved in the ¼ cup lukewarm water. Add flour, using a little more if needed to make a rather soft dough. Cover and let rise in a warm place until doubled in bulk.

Turn out on floured bo ~d and knead until smooth. Roll dough out to about ⅓ inch thick and cut in rounds with biscuit cutter. Place in greased baking pan (8 x 15), cover with a towel and let rise until doubled. Bake in 425 oven for about 15 minutes. Makes 30 to 36 rolls.

Cottage Cheese Fruit Bread

½ cup butter
⅔ cup light brown sugar
4 tsps each, grated orange & lemon rinds
2 eggs, beaten
2 cups cottage cheese
2 cups sifted flour
3 teaspoons any baking powder
1 teaspoon baking soda
1 teaspoon salt
2 cups dried currants

Cream butter and sugar together, add grated rinds. Add beaten eggs and cottage cheese and beat well. Sift dry ingredients together, mix with currants and stir into first mixture. The dough will be quite stiff. Pack dough into greased standard bread tin and bake about 1 hour in 350 oven.

Apple Bread

½ cup shortening
1 cup sugar
2 eggs, beaten
2 tablespoons sour milk
1 teaspoon vanilla
2 cups flour
1 teaspoon baking soda
1 teaspoon any baking powder
¼ teaspoon salt
2 medium apples, peeled and chopped
⅔ cup chopped nuts (optional)

Cream shortening and sugar. Add beaten eggs, sour milk and vanilla. Sift dry ingredients together and add with the chopped apple. Mix all well but do not beat. Add nuts, if desired. Bake in a greased, standard bread tin in 350 oven for about 1 hour.

Prune Bread

1 cup cooked prunes, pitted
1 cup light brown sugar, firmly packed
2 tablespoons butter, melted
1 egg, beaten
¾ cup liquid from prunes
1 cup buttermilk
1 teaspoon baking soda
½ teaspoon salt
1 teaspoon any baking powder
1 cup whole-wheat flour
1½ cups white flour

Chop prunes, add sugar, melted butter, beaten egg, prune liquid and buttermilk. Sift dry in-

gredients and combine mixtures. Mix well. Bake
in a greased standard bread tin in 325 oven for
about 1 hour and 30 minutes.

Raisin Graham Bread

1½ cups buttermilk
2 tablespoons butter, melted
⅔ cup maple syrup
2 teaspoons baking soda
½ teaspoon salt
1⅓ cups graham flour
1½ cups white flour
1 cup seeded raisins

Combine buttermilk with melted butter and
syrup. Add soda and salt. Sift white flour and
add to graham. Add flours to first mixture. Stir
in raisins. Mix well but do not beat. Pour into
greased standard bread tin and bake about 1
hour in 350 oven.

Favorite Buttermilk Biscuits

2 cups flour
1 teaspoon salt
1 teaspoon any baking powder
½ teaspoon baking soda
4 tablespoons lard
¾ cup buttermilk

Sift flour with salt, baking powder and soda. Rub
in lard. Add buttermilk and mix into a rather
soft dough, just stiff enough to be handled.
Turn out on floured board and knead slightly—
do not work as for yeast breads or the texture

will suffer. Roll out gently to about ¾ inch thick. Cut into rounds and place on greased baking pan without crowding. Bake in 425 oven about 15 minutes. Makes about 15 medium biscuits.

NOTE ABOUT BISCUITS:

It's hard to give arbitrary amounts of liquid for biscuit rules because flours differ and some will require a little more, some a little less. Just remember that dough should be rather soft.

Lard is my favorite shortening for biscuits. I've never achieved the same tenderness and lightness by using oil in a biscuit rule as I have with lard, or even some other solid shortening.

Sour-Milk Biscuits

2 cups flour
1 teaspoon salt
1 teaspoon any baking powder
½ teaspoon baking soda
4 tablespoons lard
1 cup thick sour milk

Sift dry ingredients and rub in lard. Add sour milk to make soft dough. Turn onto floured board, knead slightly and roll gently to ¾ inch thick. Cut in rounds, place without crowding on greased baking sheet. Bake in 425 oven for about 15 minutes. Makes 15.

Sweet-Milk Biscuits

2 cups flour
1 teaspoon salt
4 teaspoons any baking powder
4 tablespoons lard
¾ cup sweet milk

Sift dry ingredients, rub in lard and add milk to make soft dough. Knead sparingly on floured board and roll gently to ¾ inch thick. Cut in rounds and bake on greased baking sheet in 425 oven for about 15 minutes. Makes about 15 biscuits.

Sour-Cream Biscuits

2 cups flour
1 teaspoon salt
1 teaspoon any baking powder
½ teaspoon baking soda
1 cup sour cream

Sift dry ingredients, rub in lard, add sour cream to make soft dough. Turn out on floured board, knead sparingly and roll gently to ¾ inch thick. Cut in rounds and bake on greased sheet in 425 oven for about 15 minutes. Makes 15.

No shortening is called for in this receipt because of the fat content of the sour cream.

Biscuit Variations

Every cook had her variations of plain hot biscuits, and here are some of the best I've found.

CHEESE BISCUITS:

To any of the hot biscuit receipts, add ¾ cup diced store cheese before adding the liquid. Bake as usual. These are especially good with a cup of hot coffee.

ROLLED CINNAMON BISCUITS:

Use rule for Buttermilk Biscuits. Roll out to about ½ inch thick. Spread with ¼ cup softened butter and sprinkle with ½ cup sugar mixed with 2 teaspoons cinnamon. Roll as for jelly roll, pressing edge in place firmly but gently. Cut across roll into ¾-inch slices. Bake as for other biscuits.

MARMALADE ROLL:

Roll out as for Cinnamon Biscuits. Spread with 2 tablespoons softened butter, then thinly with orange marmalade. Roll, slice and bake as usual.

MAPLE ROLLS:

Just before baking plain biscuits, brush top of each with melted butter. Sprinkle generously with crumbled maple sugar. Bake as usual.

ORANGE TEA BISCUITS:

Just before biscuits are put in oven, place on top of each a lump of sugar which has been well soaked in orange juice. Use ordinary lump sugar. Bake as usual.

Plain Shortcake

My mother always used Sour-Cream Biscuits for her shortcakes, since there was always a good supply of this tangy liquid available, and they were excellent.

However, I've always preferred my favorite Buttermilk Biscuit rule,

If baking shortcake in one mound in a round pan, roll the dough to about 1 inch thick and bake in a 400 oven for about 18 to 20 minutes. When serving, split and butter.

Oatmeal Muffins

1½ cups milk
1 cup cooked oatmeal
2 eggs, well beaten
1 tablespoon butter, melted
1⅔ cups flour
3 teaspoons any baking powder
½ teaspoon salt
2 tablespoons sugar

Scald milk and add oatmeal. Add beaten eggs and melted butter. Sift flour with baking powder, salt and sugar and add to milk mixture. Don't beat, just stir enough to mix. Fill greased muffin cups about ⅔ full and bake in 400 oven for about 20 minutes. Makes 12 to 15 muffins.

Apple Muffins

    1 egg, beaten
    4 tablespoons shortening, melted
    ½ cup sugar
    2 cups flour
    4 teaspoons any baking powder
    ½ teaspoon salt
    1 cup milk
    2 medium apples, peeled and chopped
    2 teaspoons sugar for topping
    ¼ teaspoon cinnamon for topping

Add shortening and sugar to beaten egg. Sift dry ingredients together and add to first mixture alternately with milk. Add apple. Do not beat, just stir until ingredients are mixed. Fill greased muffin cups about ⅔ full and sprinkle the mixed sugar and cinnamon over tops. Bake in 375 oven for about 20 minutes. Makes about 9 large muffins.

Rice Cornmeal Muffins

    1¼ cups cooked rice
    1 cup cornmeal
    2 tablespoons sugar
    2 tablespoons butter, melted
    1 teaspoon salt
    2 teaspoons baking powder
    1 scant cup milk
    2 eggs

Mix sugar and butter. Separate eggs, beat egg yolks well and add. Stir in milk, then add rice.

Sift dry ingredients and stir into first mixture. Beat egg whites stiff and fold into batter. Fill greased muffin cups about ⅔ full. Bake in 375 oven for about 25 minutes. Makes about 15 muffins.

Apple Johnnycake

    2 cups cornmeal
    ¼ cup sugar
    1 teaspoon salt
    2 cups sour milk (or buttermilk)
    2 tablespoons butter, melted
    2 eggs, beaten
    1 teaspoon baking soda
    1 tablespoon cold water
    2 medium apples, peeled and chopped

Mix cornmeal, sugar, salt, sour milk and melted butter. Cook over hot water for about 10 minutes. Cool, then add beaten eggs and soda, which has been dissolved in the cold water. Mix all well. Add chopped apple. Bake in square greased cake pan (about 9 x 9) for about 30 minutes in a 400 oven. Serves 6 to 8.

Custard Johnnycake

    1½ cups cornmeal
    ½ cup flour
    2 tablespoons sugar
    1 teaspoon baking powder
    1 teaspoon baking soda
    1 teaspoon salt
    2 eggs, beaten

    1 cup buttermilk
    2 cups sweet milk
    3 tablespoons butter, melted

Sift dry ingredients together. Add beaten eggs to 1 cup of the sweet milk and the 1 cup buttermilk, and add to cornmeal mixture. Add melted butter. Pour into greased pan, and pour the remaining 1 cup sweet milk into the center of the batter. *Don't tip pan or stir batter again.* Bake in 400 oven for about 30 minutes.

Old-time cooks liked to use their cast-iron spider (about 10 inches across) as a baking pan for custard johnnycake, but if your frying pans have handles that will not stand oven temperatures, use a round cake pan of approximately the same diameter.

Cut johnnycake in pie-shaped pieces and serve hot with butter. Custard johnnycake will not be as light as ordinary cornbread, but I prefer its delicious texture. This is another very old recipe, and a favorite one of many old people, who remember it from their childhood.

Buttermilk Popovers

    1¼ cups buttermilk
    1 cup flour
    ¾ teaspoon salt
    1 teaspoon sugar
    1 tablespoon butter, melted
    2 eggs
    1 teaspoon any baking powder

Beat flour into buttermilk until free from lumps.

Add salt, sugar and melted butter. Separate eggs, beat yolks well and add. Continue beating until smooth. Let stand while you grease and heat an iron popover pan. Whip egg whites stiff, beating into them the baking powder. Fold into first mixture. Fill each popover cup full and bake for 10 minutes in 400 oven. Reduce heat to 350 and bake 15 or 20 minutes longer.

These popovers are extremely light and will have a tiny bit of soft custard inside. They should be eaten piping hot from the oven, although I've discovered they will stand a few minutes without falling. Makes about 12 popovers.

Old-Fashioned Bread Doughnuts

2 cups sponge (from White Bread)
1 egg, well beaten
½ cup shortening, melted
1 cup warm milk
½ cup sugar
about 3 cups flour
¼ teaspoon nutmeg (optional)
deep fat for frying

When bread sponge is light and bubbly, take out 2 cups before you add more flour to finish your bread.

To the 2 cups of sponge add the egg, melted shortening, the 1 cup warm milk and the sugar. Mix well and stir in enough flour to make a smooth, soft dough—it is impossible to give an arbitrary amount of flour needed, because bread sponges vary widely in their consistency. Add nutmeg with flour, if desired.

Cover, let rise until doubled, then turn out on floured board. Knead, roll out about ½ inch thick, cut with doughnut cutter, then cover with a towel and let rise about 1 hour in a warm place. Fry in deep hot fat, the same as for any doughnut according to the method below. Drain on brown paper. Makes about 30 to 36.

This is the old-time way of making raised doughnuts. It was a simple matter to begin with bread sponge and go on from there. These doughnuts were always served at sugaring-off parties, with a huge sour pickle to provide the contrast needed to offset the sweetness of maple syrup or sugar-on-snow.

FRYING DOUGHNUTS:

Heat lard, shortening or oil to 370 degrees. How much lard or other fat you will need depends upon the size of your frying kettle, but in general you should have at least 2 pounds to start off with. If you have no thermometer to test fat temperature, drop one 1-inch cube of bread into fat. If it browns in 1 minute, the temperature is right for frying doughnuts or fritters. Keep fat at even heat, because doughnuts may soak fat if it cools.

Slide doughnuts into hot fat very carefully, either with fingers or with a spatula. Don't try to fry more than four at a time. When brown on one side, turn and brown on the other. Turn only once. Take from fat with a long cooking fork, and drain on brown paper or paper towel.

Do not stick fork into doughnut while taking from fat. If level of fat drops below 2 inches from top of kettle, add more cold fat and wait until all is proper temperature again.

Raised Doughnuts

> 1 cup milk, scalded
> ¼ cup shortening, melted
> ¾ cup light brown sugar
> 1 teaspoon salt
> 1 yeast cake (or envelope)
> ¼ cup lukewarm water
> about 3 cups flour
> pinch of nutmeg (optional)
> 2 eggs, beaten
> deep fat for frying

Add sugar, salt and shortening to hot milk. Cool to lukewarm and add the yeast dissolved in the ¼ cup lukewarm water. Stir in about 1½ cups of the flour to make a smooth batter. Cover and let rise in a warm place until sponge is light and bubbly, about 1 hour. Stir in eggs, and the remaining flour sifted with the nutmeg, to make a rather soft dough, adding a little more flour if necessary. Turn out on floured board, knead, then return to bowl, cover and let rise again until doubled. Turn out on floured board, knead down, roll to about ½ inch thick. Cut with doughnut cutter, cover with towel and let rise about 1 hour. Fry according to method given with Old-Fashioned Bread Doughnuts. Makes about 36.

Buttermilk Doughnuts

2 eggs, well beaten
1 cup sugar
2 tablespoons butter, melted
1 cup buttermilk (or sour milk)
1 teaspoon soda
1 teaspoon any baking powder
1 teaspoon salt
about 4 cups flour
deep fat for frying

Combine beaten eggs, sugar and melted butter, then buttermilk. Sift 3 cups of the flour with the dry ingredients and add to first mixture. Add gradually just enough more of the flour to make a dough soft but firm enough to handle. Roll out to about ⅓ inch thick. Cut out and fry in deep, hot fat until brown on both sides, turning only once. (*See* method given with Old-Fashioned Bread Doughnuts.) Makes about 40 doughnuts.

Vermont Fritters

1 cup sour milk
½ teaspoon baking soda
1 egg, beaten
about 2 cups flour
¼ teaspoon salt
deep fat for frying

Dissolve soda in sour milk and add to egg. Sift flour with the salt and add to first mixture. Batter should be a little stiffer than muffin batter. Drop from teaspoon into deep, hot fat as for Old-Fashioned Bread Doughnuts, browning on one side, then turning quickly with fork. Drain on brown paper and serve warm with maple syrup. Makes about 30.

These fritters were an indispensable accompaniment to new maple syrup in sugaring season.

Buttermilk Pancakes

2 eggs, beaten
2 cups buttermilk
2 cups flour
1 tablespoon sugar
½ teaspoon baking soda
½ teaspoon salt
2 teaspoons any baking powder
1 tablespoon shortening, melted

Add beaten eggs to buttermilk. Sift dry ingredients together and combine mixtures. Add melted shortening. Do not beat batter. Bake on hot, greased griddle, turning only once. When bubbles appear on top of cake, turn carefully and brown on other side. Sour milk may be used instead of buttermilk. Will make 15 to 20 medium pancakes.

Serve hot with butter and maple syrup. Serve from griddle, if possible. Otherwise, pancakes may be kept hot until all are baked by buttering lightly and stacking on hot platter in oven turned on very low heat, the door propped open a few inches.

Sweet-Milk Griddlecakes

1⅞ cups sweet milk
2 eggs, beaten
2 cups flour
4 teaspoons baking powder
2 tablespoons sugar
1 teaspoon salt
2 tablespoons shortening, melted

Add beaten eggs to milk. Sift dry ingredients together and add to milk mixture, mixing only enough to moisten all ingredients. Add in melted shortening, but do not beat (texture toughens if beaten). Bake on greased hot griddle, turning only once. When bubbles appear on top of pancake, turn carefully and bake on other side. Serve hot with butter and maple syrup. Makes 15 to 20 medium griddlecakes.

Pancake Variations

Pancakes, either sweet-milk, sour-milk or buttermilk, are extremely versatile in that many different additions may be made to the batter, all excellent. Here are some of the best ones. The addition of any of these doesn't materially change the yield, perhaps an increase of 1 or 2 medium pancakes. Serve as usual, with butter and syrup.

BLUEBERRY PANCAKES:

Add 1 cup washed and drained blueberries to batter and bake as usual.

APPLE GRIDDLECAKES:

Peel and slice thin 1 medium tart apple and add to batter.

BACON OR SAUSAGE PANCAKES:

Add 1 cup of chopped, cooked bacon or sausage, well drained, to batter.

CORN PANCAKES:

Add 1 cup of drained whole-kernel corn to make an excellent pancake.

Old-Fashioned Buckwheat Griddlecakes

    1 yeast cake (or envelope)
    1/3 cup lukewarm water
    1/2 cup cornmeal
    3/4 cup boiling water
    1 1/2 cups buckwheat flour
    1 cup buttermilk
    1/2 teaspoon soda
    1/2 teaspoon salt
    1 tablespoon light molasses

Dissolve yeast in warm water. Stir cornmeal into boiling water, add buttermilk and buckwheat flour. Cool to lukewarm, then add yeast and stir all into a smooth, rather thin batter. Cover and let stand in a warm place overnight. It will be light and bubbly in the morning and have a nice, yeasty smell.

In the morning, add salt and molasses. Batter

should be rather thick, yet of a consistency to pour from a pitcher (the favorite method of old-time cooks). If batter appears too thick, a little sweet milk may be added. Pour or drop batter onto hot greased griddle. Bake as usual, turning only once. Serve hot with butter and maple syrup. Makes about 20 medium griddle-cakes.

Many cooks of bygone years kept their raised buckwheat-cake batter going all Winter. A cup of the batter, reserved from each batch, started the batter for the next day, if kept at room temperature so that the yeast bubbles never stopped forming. I'm sure the fragrance of those hot buckwheat cakes penetrated into every corner of the house and was sufficient inducement to hurry down to breakfast before the griddle-cakes had a chance to cool.

Breadcrumb Griddlecakes

1½ cups soft breadcrumbs
1 cup flour
1 teaspoon salt
3 teaspoons any baking powder
1 teaspoon sugar
2 cups milk
2 eggs
3 tablespoons butter, melted

Scald 1 cup of the milk and soak breadcrumbs in it. Cool. Sift dry ingredients together. Separate eggs, beat yolks and add to other cup of milk. Pour into breadcrumb mixture, then combine with the dry ingredients, blending but *not* beating. Add melted butter, then fold in stiffly beaten egg whites. Bake on hot greased griddle, turning only once. Will make 15 to 20 medium cakes. Serve very hot with butter and maple syrup.

Rice Pancakes

1 cup leftover cooked rice
½ cup flour
1½ teaspoons baking powder
1 teaspoon salt
1 teaspoon sugar
2 eggs
1 cup milk
2 tablespoons butter, melted

Separate eggs, beat yolks, then add milk and butter. Beat well. Sift dry ingredients together and add to egg mixture. Add rice. Beat egg whites stiff and fold into batter. Drop from spoon onto hot greased griddle. Brown on under side, turn quickly when cake appears full of air bubbles, and brown on other side. Will make about 12 medium-sized pancakes.

These pancakes should be served sizzling hot with butter and maple syrup.

Thin Dessert Pancakes

1 cup flour
3 tablespoons sugar
½ teaspoon salt
1 cup milk
2 eggs, beaten
confectioner's sugar for dusting
jelly

Mix flour with sugar and salt, add milk and stir until smooth and free from lumps. Beat eggs, add and beat all thoroughly. Drop from tablespoon to hot greased griddle, using about 3 table-spoonsful for each cake. Spread batter evenly by tilting griddle immediately after dropping batter. When brown on one side, turn quickly and brown on other. Cakes will be thin, so will cook in about 1 minute for each side.

Spread each pancake with a tart jelly—such as grape—roll and serve at once. A light dusting of confectioner's sugar over each roll adds to the attractive appearance of the pancake rolls. Will make 12 to 18 pancakes, depending upon size.

These thin and tender pancakes may be used in any recipe requiring a sweet pancake that may be rolled.

CHAPTER SEVEN

Cakes and Cookies

PRESENT-DAY CAKES doubtless bear little resemblance to those of a hundred and fifty years ago, a fact not too surprising when one considers that until fairly recently there was no soft, feathery cake flour or creamy white, delicately flavored shortening. The best cakes then were made of butter, cream and eggs, of course—but any cook knows that the flour has a great deal to do with the texture of her cake.

There were several cakes, however, that made good use of the ingredients at hand. Dark chocolate layer cake made with sour milk needs no apology, nor do a certain fruitcake calling for dried apples and a prune cake that's just about the best thing you've ever eaten. And many cooks prided themselves, and justly so, on their wonderful maple layer cakes, high and round, studded with butternuts.

Cookies were a different story, and the old

receipts supply us with a wide variety of treats qualified to take their place in any good cook's kitchen. The materials abundant on the hill farm were, happily, well suited to cookie making: perhaps that's why the back-pantry cookie jar was outsize and never empty.

NOTE: More rules for cakes and cookies will be found in Chapter Nine, *Maple Sugar and Maple Syrup.*

Dark Chocolate Layer Cake

2⅔ cups light brown sugar, well packed
⅔ cup softened butter
3 egg yolks
1 whole egg
4 ounces baking chocolate (unsweetened)
⅔ cup boiled water
2⅔ cups sifted flour
1½ teaspoons any baking powder
pinch of salt
⅔ cup sour milk
1¼ teaspoons baking soda
1 teaspoon vanilla
about 2½ cups Dark Chocolate Frosting

Cream brown sugar with the butter, beating well. Add egg yolks and the whole egg, beating very well. Melt chocolate in the boiling water, stirring until smooth and thick. Add to first mixture. Sift flour with salt and baking powder. Dissolve soda in the sour milk and add to chocolate mixture alternately with flour mixture. Beat all well. Add vanilla. Bake in 2 greased layer-cake pans for 25 to 30 minutes in 350 oven. Cool. Put together with Dark Chocolate Frosting between layers and over top.

DARK CHOCOLATE FROSTING:

3 ounces baking chocolate (unsweetened)
2 tablespoons butter
1 egg, beaten
½ cup milk
1 cup granulated sugar
1 teaspoon vinegar
1 teaspoon vanilla
about 3 cups confectioner's sugar

Melt the chocolate over hot water. Add the butter, egg, milk and granulated sugar. Cook over very low heat until thickened, about 5 minutes, stirring constantly. Set aside to cool, then add the vinegar and vanilla. Stir in the confectioner's sugar to make right consistency to spread. Makes about 2½ cups.

This is a smooth, creamy frosting and well worth the little more trouble it requires.

Light Chocolate Potato Cake

2 medium potatoes, peeled
1 ounce baking chocolate (unsweetened)
1 cup shortening, softened
2 cups sugar
2 teaspoons grated lemon rind
4 eggs, well beaten
½ cup milk
2 cups sifted flour
½ teaspoon salt
2 teaspoons any baking powder

Boil potatoes until tender, drain and put through ricer. Set aside 1 cup of the riced potatoes to cool. Melt chocolate and set aside to cool. Cream shortening with sugar and lemon rind, beating well. Add beaten eggs, then stir in the melted chocolate. Add milk to the 1 cup of riced potato. Sift flour with salt and baking powder and add alternately with potato mixture to chocolate mixture. Beat until batter is smooth. Pour into 2 greased layer-cake pans and bake in 350 oven for about 45 minutes. Cool and use any desired frosting between layers and over top and sides.

Cream Cake

2 eggs
1 cup sugar
1 cup heavy sweet cream
2 cups flour
1/4 teaspoon salt
2 teaspoons cream of tartar
1 teaspoon baking soda
1 teaspoon lemon extract

Separate eggs and beat yolks well, then beat in the sugar. Sift dry ingredients together and add alternately with the cream. Add lemon extract. Beat egg whites until stiff and fold into batter. Bake in 2 greased layer-cake pans in 375 oven for about 25 minutes. Use any desired frosting between layers and over top and sides of cake.

This recipe was a great favorite on farms where the supply of cream was plentiful and other shortening often lacking.

Dried Apple Fruitcake

3 cups dried apples
3 cups light molasses
1 cup seeded raisins
3 cups flour
1 cup shortening, well softened
3 eggs, beaten
1 teaspoon baking soda
1 teaspoon salt
1 teaspoon cinnamon
½ teaspoon nutmeg
¼ teaspoon cloves

Soak apples overnight in just enough water to cover. In the morning, cut apples quite fine, add molasses and cook gently until apples are very tender. Add raisins and cook 5 minutes more. Remove from heat, cool, then add shortening and eggs. Sift dry ingredients together and add to previous mixture. Blend well, then pour into 2 greased standard bread tins. Bake in 350 oven for about 1 hour.

This old-time cake is delicious. The bits of apple taste like citron.

Old-Fashioned Pork Cake

½ cup finely ground fat salt pork
½ cup boiling water
½ teaspoon baking soda
½ cup light molasses
1 cup sugar
2 eggs, beaten
about 1½ cups flour
½ teaspoon cinnamon

½ teaspoon cloves
½ teaspoon nutmeg
½ cup chopped citron
1 cup seeded raisins

Pour boiling water over the salt pork. Cool, then add the soda, molasses and sugar. Beat in the eggs. Sift 1 cup of the flour with the spices and add to previous mixture with the citron and raisins. Mix, then sift in remaining flour to make a rather stiff batter (like any fruitcake). Since flours differ in texture, a little more or less than the amount given may be needed. Pour into a greased, standard bread tin and bake in 300 oven for about 1 hour and 30 minutes.

This is another very old cake and is so good many New England women still make it. It is an excellent keeper if well wrapped in waxed paper and stored in a covered container.

Filled Prune Cake

¾ cup butter
1 cup sugar
1 cup mashed cooked prunes (½ pound dried)
1¼ cups flour
1 teaspoon baking soda
1 teaspoon cinnamon
½ teaspoon nutmeg
½ teaspoon cloves
3 tablespoons sour cream
3 eggs, beaten
1½ cups Raisin-Nut Filling
2 cups Seven-Minute White Frosting

Cream   butter and sugar, add prunes, which

should be well drained. Sift dry ingredients together and add to prune mixture with sour cream and beaten eggs. Blend well and bake in 2 greased layer-cake pans in a 350 oven for about 30 minutes. Cool layers and put together with filling, and frost.

RAISIN-NUT FILLING:

> 1 beaten egg
> ½ cup sugar
> ½ cup sour cream
> ½ cup chopped nutmeats
> 1 cup chopped seeded raisins

Mix all together and cook over hot water until thick, about 5 minutes, stirring constantly. Cool and spread between layers. Makes about 1½ cups.

SEVEN-MINUTE WHITE FROSTING:

> 1½ cups sugar
> 4 tablespoons water
> ¼ teaspoon cream of tartar
> 2 egg whites, unbeaten
> 1 teaspoon vanilla

Place sugar, water, cream of tartar and egg whites in top of double boiler. Cook over boiling water until thick and smooth, beating constantly with egg beater. When frosting is stiff enough to stand in peaks, remove from heat, add vanilla and beat until smooth, 1 minute more. Spread at once on cake before frosting cools.

If an electric beater is used, cooking time will probably be a little shortened, to about 5 or 6 minutes. Makes about 2 cups.

Blackberry Jam Cake

⅔ cup butter, softened
1 cup sugar
3 eggs, well beaten
1 cup blackberry jam
¼ cup black coffee
4 tablespoons sour cream
2½ cups sifted flour
1 teaspoon any baking powder
1 teaspoon baking soda
pinch of salt
1 teaspoon cinnamon
½ teaspoon ground cloves
about 2½ cups Mocha Frosting

Cream butter and sugar. Add egg and jam and beat well. Sift dry ingredients together and add to first mixture alternately with sour cream and coffee. Beat all well. Pour into 2 greased layer-cake pans and bake in 350 oven for about 30 minutes. Cool layers and put together with Mocha Frosting between layers and spread over top and sides.

Raspberry jam may be used instead of blackberry.

MOCHA FROSTING:

2 egg whites
1½ cups granulated sugar
4 tablespoons cold strong coffee
¼ teaspoon cream of tartar
1 teaspoon vanilla

Place egg whites, sugar, cream of tartar and coffee in top of double boiler and cook over boiling water, beating constantly with an egg beater until frosting will stand in peaks, 5 to 7 minutes. Remove from heat, add vanilla and beat until smooth, 1 minute more. Spread immediately on cooled cake. Will make about 2½ cups.

If an electric beater is used, the cooking time may be shorter, perhaps as little as 4 minutes.

Poor Man's Fruitcake

2 cups light brown sugar, well packed
2 cups hot water
1 package seeded raisins (about 2¾ cups)
2 tablespoons lard
1 teaspoon cinnamon
1 teaspoon ground cloves
1 teaspoon baking soda
about 3 cups flour
1 teaspoon salt
1 cup broken nutmeats (optional)

Add sugar, raisins, lard and spices to the hot water and boil together for 5 minutes. Remove from heat, cool, then dissolve soda in the liquid. Add about 3 cups flour, sifted with the salt. If using nutmeats, add with the flour. Stir well and bake in large bread tin (about 5 x 12) in 325 oven for about 1 hour and 15 minutes.

This cake is as good as it is economical and will keep for weeks, if well wrapped in waxed paper and stored in a covered container.

Molasses Filled Cookies

about 2 cups Date-Raisin Filling
1 cup sugar
1 egg, beaten
¾ cup lard, melted
¼ cup hot water
½ cup light molasses
1 teaspoon baking soda
½ teaspoon cinnamon
¼ teaspoon nutmeg
¼ teaspoon cloves
½ teaspoon salt
about 4 cups flour

Cream sugar with the egg. Add melted lard and hot water, then molasses. Sift soda, spices and the salt with 1 cup of the flour. Stir into first mixture. Add remaining flour to make a firm dough, stiff enough to handle and roll easily, adding more flour if needed. Roll to about ¼ inch thick, cut with round cutter about 2½ inches in diameter. Put 1 rounded teaspoon of the filling in center of one cookie and cover with another, pinching the edges together carefully and pricking center of top cookie with a fork. Place on greased cookie sheet and bake in 400 oven for about 15 minutes. Makes about 4 dozen.

These are among the most delicious and satisfactory cookies I've come across. The dough will keep several days in the refrigerator if well covered. (I've often kept it as long as a week, and have found it a lifesaver to be able to serve freshly baked cookies with less than a half-hour's notice).

I often have a small amount of the filling left over, but this is no problem since it will keep almost indefinitely in a covered jar in the refrigerator. Whether or not you have too much filling for the amount of dough depends on how thin you roll the dough, the size of your cutter and how full you like your cookies filled. Incidentally, this leftover filling, with cream cheese as a partner, makes an excellent afternoon tea sandwich with thin white bread.

DATE-RAISIN FILLING:

> 1 cup pitted dates, well packed
> 1 cup seeded raisins, well packed
> ½ cup sugar
> ¾ cup water
> 4 teaspoons flour
> 1 teaspoon vanilla

Put dates and raisins through food grinder. Add rest of ingredients. Cook over low heat until thick, about 3 minutes, stirring so that filling does not scorch. Cool before using. Makes about 2 cups.

Railroad Cookies

> about 2½ cups Date-Nut Filling
> 1 cup shortening
> 2 cups brown sugar, well packed
> 2 eggs, beaten
> 1 teaspoon baking soda
> ¼ teaspoon salt
> 1 teaspoon cinnamon
> about 4 cups flour

Cream sugar and shortening. Beat in the eggs. Sift soda, salt and cinnamon with 2 cups of the flour. Stir into first mixture, then add remaining flour to make a firm dough, stiff enough to handle and roll easily. Dough will be easier to handle if divided into 2 parts before rolling. Roll out each half of dough about ⅓ inch thick and spread with the date filling. Roll up like a jelly roll. Chill well, then slice crosswise into thin slices, about ¼ inch thick. Bake on greased cookie sheets in 350 oven for about 15 minutes. Makes 3 to 4 dozen.

This is a very easy cookie to make, since cookies are sliced rather than cut out. The rolled cookie dough will keep for a week if well wrapped in waxed paper and stored in the refrigerator.

The origin of this cookie's name is lost in time, but my mother told me it was because people of years ago fancied the dark track of the filling curving through the golden cookie resembled the railroad tracks winding up through the valleys and hills.

DATE-NUT FILLING:

    2 cups pitted dates, chopped very fine
    ½ cup sugar
    ½ cup water
    1 teaspoon vanilla
    1 tablespoon butter
    ½ cup ground nutmeats

Cook dates, sugar and water together over low heat until thick, about 3 minutes, stirring to prevent scorching. Add vanilla and butter. Cool and add nutmeats, which have been put through coarse knife of food grinder. Makes about 2½ cups.

Pumpkin Cookies

⅓ cup shortening
1 cup sugar
2 eggs
1 teaspoon vanilla
1 teaspoon lemon extract
1 cup cooked mashed pumpkin
2½ cups flour
4 teaspoons any baking powder
¼ teaspoon salt
¼ teaspoon ginger
¼ teaspoon nutmeg
1 cup seeded raisins
½ cup chopped nutmeats

Cream sugar with shortening and eggs. Beat well, add vanilla and lemon extract. Stir in pumpkin, which has been mashed smooth and fine. Sift dry ingredients together and add with raisins and nuts. Mix well. Drop by teaspoon onto greased cookie sheet and bake about 15 minutes in 375 oven. Makes about 4 dozen.

Apple Butter Cookies

¼ cup shortening
⅔ cup light brown sugar, well packed
1 egg, beaten
¼ cup apple butter
1 cup flour

½ teaspoon baking soda
½ teaspoon any baking powder
½ teaspoon salt
2 tablespoons milk
1 cup uncooked oatmeal
½ cup chopped nutmeats
½ cup seedless raisins, chopped

Cream shortening and sugar. Beat in egg, then apple butter. Sift together the flour, soda, baking powder and salt and add with the milk to first mixture. Mix well, then add the oatmeal, nuts and raisins. Drop from teaspoon onto greased cookie sheet and bake about 15 minutes in 375 oven. Makes about 3 dozen.

Prune Cookies

¾ cup pitted cooked prunes, drained
⅓ cup shortening
1 cup brown sugar, well packed
1 egg, beaten
¼ cup sour milk
1 teaspoon vanilla
½ teaspoon baking soda
½ teaspoon any baking powder
pinch of salt
1¾ cups flour
1 teaspoon cinnamon
⅓ cup chopped nutmeats

Chop prunes fine. Cream shortening and sugar, beat in egg, sour milk and vanilla. Stir in prunes. Sift dry ingredients together and add with the nuts. Drop from teaspoon onto greased cookie sheet and bake about 15 minutes in 350 oven. Cookies will be soft and puffy. Makes about 3½ dozen.

Oatmeal Fruit Cookies

⅔ cup shortening, softened
1 cup sugar
2 eggs, beaten
1½ cups flour
½ teaspoon baking soda
½ teaspoon salt
2 teaspoons ground cinnamon
½ cup milk
1½ cups uncooked oatmeal
1 cup seedless raisins
½ cup chopped nutmeats

Cream shortening with the sugar, then beat in the eggs. Sift the flour with the soda, salt and cinnamon, and add to first mixture with the ½ cup milk. Mix well, then stir in oatmeal, raisins and nuts. Drop from teaspoon onto greased cookie sheet and bake in 400 oven for about 15 minutes. Makes about 4 dozen.

This recipe makes a soft, sweet cookie, in my opinion one much better than the ordinary firm oatmeal cookie.

Raisin Spice Cookies

1 cup seeded raisins
½ cup raisin water
1 cup light brown sugar
1 egg, beaten
½ cup shortening, softened
1 teaspoon baking soda
2¼ cups flour
½ teaspoon cinnamon
¼ teaspoon ground cloves
¼ teaspoon nutmeg
pinch of salt

Simmer raisins for 20 minutes in water barely covering. Drain well and reserve ½ cup of the water. Cream shortening, sugar and egg together, mixing well. Sift baking soda with flour, spices and salt and add to first mixture alternately with raisin water. Add raisins. Drop from teaspoon onto greased cookie sheet and bake about 15 minutes in 375 oven. Makes about 4 dozen.

Iced Ginger Cream Cookies

½ cup light brown sugar
½ cup light molasses
½ cup shortening, softened
½ cup buttermilk
1 teaspoon cinnamon
1 teaspoon ginger
1 teaspoon baking soda
3½ cups flour
about ⅔ cup Thin Water Icing

Cream shortening and sugar, add molasses and buttermilk, then add soda dissolved in a little hot water. Sift dry ingredients and add. Roll out about ¼ inch thick, cut and place on greased cookie sheet. Bake in 350 oven for about 10 minutes. Cool and frost lightly with Thin Water Icing. Makes about 3 dozen.

THIN WATER ICING:

    2 tablespoons cold water

    about 1½ cups confectioner's sugar

    ½ teaspoon vanilla

Put water in a bowl and stir in sugar gradually until smooth. Icing should be fairly thin, not as thick as for frosting a cake. Add vanilla. Spread with broad-bladed knife. Do not frost cookies too heavily. Makes about ⅔ cup.

Butternut Balls

    ½ cup butter

    5 tablespoons sugar

    1 egg

    1 teaspoon grated lemon rind

    1 tablespoon lemon juice

    1 teaspoon vanilla

    1½ cups ground butternuts

    1⅛ cups flour

    ½ cup powdered sugar for rolling

Cream sugar and butter. Separate egg. Beat yolk and add lemon rind, lemon juice and vanilla. Combine with sugar and butter mixture. Sift flour and mix with 1 cup of the ground butternuts. Add to previous mixture. Dough will be stiff. Form small balls with fingers.

Beat the egg white until frothy but not stiff and dip each ball in it, then roll in the powdered sugar, which has been mixed with the remaining ½ cup of ground butternuts. Place on greased cookie sheet and bake about 15 minutes in 375 oven.

This will make about 3 dozen small balls, very rich and very good. Walnuts may be used instead of butternuts.

Old-Fashioned Caraway Cookies

        1 cup sour cream
        1 teaspoon baking soda
        ¾ cup shortening, softened
        2 cups sugar
        2 eggs, beaten
        1 teaspoon vanilla
        about 4½ cups flour
        2 tablespoons caraway seeds for topping
        ¼ cup sugar for topping

Add soda to the sour cream. Cream shortening with the sugar, then add eggs, beating well. Add sour-cream mixture to egg-and-shortening mixture. Sift flour and add. Dough should be stiff enough to handle and roll easily. Roll out to about ¼ inch thick and cut. Sprinkle with the ¼ cup sugar, then sprinkle sparingly with the .caraway seeds; the amount used will depend upon individual tastes, since caraway has a quite decided flavor. Place cookies on a greased cookie sheet and bake in 350 oven for about 10 to 12 minutes. Makes 4 to 5 dozen.

Cottage Cheese Cookies

½ cup butter (or lard)
1½ cups sugar
2 eggs
2½ tablespoons lemon juice
2 teaspoons grated lemon rind
1 cup cottage cheese
2 cups flour
1 teaspoon any baking powder
1 teaspoon salt

Cream butter with sugar until fluffy. Beat in eggs, lemon juice and rind. Put cottage cheese through sieve and add to batter, beating well. Sift dry ingredients together, add to first mixture and mix thoroughly. Drop from teaspoon onto greased cookie tin. Bake in 400 oven for about 15 minutes. Makes around 4 dozen.

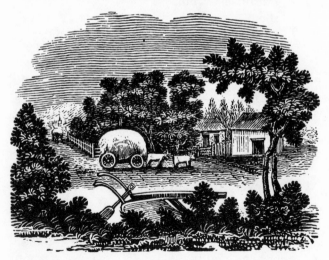

CHAPTER EIGHT

Puddings and Pies

EVERY OLD COLLECTION of favorite recipes boasted a variety of puddings, since the materials particularly suited to making these desserts—eggs and apples, maple sugar and syrup, milk, butter and cream—abounded in Yankee hill country. And there must have been many other rules for delectable puddings that were never written down at all.

A week's supply of pies was usually made on Saturday and stored on a high shelf in the back pantry. Mince and apple, pumpkin and raisin were the standbys because they kept well. In Winter the keeping was no problem, though, for the pies froze solid in the unheated back pantry almost as soon as they were put there, to be brought in as needed and set on the shelf of the black-iron cookstove to thaw.

Early Winter found the cellar full of "pie timber"—as the old people called it: barrels of apples and jars of mincemeat, both green-tomato and the real stuff made of beef and suet; there was a mound of yellow pumpkins in a corner, and raisins were easily had from the village store.

But by Spring the pumpkins had long since been used. The barrels of apples were reduced to a few dry and shriveled remnants. The mincemeat was gone, too. But pies still had to be made. I wonder who was clever enough to think of some of those old receipts—ones that must go back to the days of the early settlers in the mountains? And who but a farmwife in the wilderness would have had the ingenuity to make such good food from such unlikely materials?

NOTE: More rules for puddings and pies will be found in Chapter Nine, *Maple Sugar and Maple Syrup*.

Spiced Crumb Pudding

    1 cup dry breadcrumbs
    1 cup sour milk
    ¼ cup butter, softened
    1 cup light brown sugar
    2 tablespoons light molasses
    ½ cup sifted flour
    ½ teaspoon ground cloves
    ½ teaspoon cinnamon
    1 teaspoon baking soda
    ¾ cup seeded raisins
    1 cup whipping cream for topping

Soak crumbs in sour milk for about 1 hour. Cream butter and sugar, add molasses and beat well. Sift dry ingredients and add to butter mixture. Add raisins and soaked crumbs. Beat all well. Bake in buttered baking dish for about 45 minutes in 375 oven. Serve hot or cold, with whipped cream sweetened to taste. Will serve 7 to 8.

Spice Puffs with Peaches

⅓ cup butter, softened
1 cup light brown sugar
1 egg, beaten
1 teaspoon vanilla
2 cups sifted flour
1 teaspoon baking soda
1½ teaspoons cinnamon
½ teaspoon ground cloves
¼ teaspoon nutmeg
pinch of salt
1 cup sour milk
1 cup chopped canned peaches, drained
½ cup whipping cream for topping

Cream butter and sugar, add vanilla and egg, beating well. Sift dry ingredients together and add alternately with the sour milk to the first mixture. Beat all well and bake in greased muffin tin, filling each cup about ½ full. Bake in 375 oven for about 15 minutes. Makes 15 or 16 puffs.

To serve, scoop out the top of each puff, put a tablespoonful of chopped canned peaches in each hollow, replace top and decorate with about a teaspoon of whipped cream, sweetened to taste. They're delicious!

Apple Bread Pudding

5 slices stale white bread
2 cups applesauce, sweetened to taste
⅛ teaspoon cinnamon
pinch of nutmeg
2 tablespoons butter
2 cups milk
2 eggs, beaten
½ cup sugar
pinch of salt
½ teaspoon vanilla

Break bread into small pieces, not crumbs. Put half in bottom of buttered deep baking dish. Add cinnamon and nutmeg to applesauce and spread over bread in dish, then cover with remaining bread. Dot with the butter. Mix milk, eggs, sugar, salt and vanilla and pour over bread. Bake in 325 oven for about 1 hour or until pudding is puffed and set. Serve warm with unwhipped sweet cream. Serves 6 to 8.

Bird's Nest Pudding

4 large tart apples
½ cup seeded raisins
4 eggs, beaten
1 cup sugar
pinch of nutmeg
pinch of salt
3 cups milk

Pare and core apples. Place upright in buttered baking dish. Fill holes in apples with the raisins.

Mix eggs, sugar, salt, nutmeg and milk and pour over apples. Bake in 325 oven until apples are tender and custard looks curdled, about 45 minutes. Serves 4 to 6.

This very old pudding has a curious name and appearance but it possesses a delightful flavor.

Poor Man's Rice Pudding

1 tablespoon rice
1 tablespoon sugar
½ teaspoon cinnamon
4 cups milk
pinch of salt

Combine ingredients and pour into buttered baking dish. Bake about 5 hours in a 200 oven. During first half of baking, stir from time to time, but do not stir during the last half. The oven must be so slow that only a faintly brown top is made. May be eaten hot or cold. Serves 6.

This old-fashioned pudding is wonderfully creamy and good. It will have a delicate pink color when done. The long, slow cooking is the secret of this pudding's quality—also many cooks have to try it before they're convinced that only 1 tablespoon each of rice and sugar are required!

Cornmeal Custard Pudding

2½ tablespoons cornmeal
2 tablespoons light molasses
¾ cup sugar
¼ teaspoon salt
¼ teaspoon cinnamon
2 cups milk
2 eggs
½ cup whipping cream (optional)

Combine cornmeal, molasses, sugar, salt, cinnamon and milk. Separate eggs. Beat yolks and add to milk mixture. Beat egg whites stiff and fold into batter. Bake in greased pudding dish for about 45 minutes in 350 oven. Serves 6.

Serve warm with whipped cream, sweetened to taste, or with unwhipped cream. It is very good served with no cream at all.

Steamed Carrot Pudding

1 cup grated raw carrots (about 3 medium)
1 cup grated raw potatoes (about 2 medium)
1 teaspoon baking soda
½ cup butter, melted
1 cup brown sugar
1½ cups flour
1 teaspoon salt
1 teaspoon cinnamon
½ teaspoon nutmeg
½ teaspoon ground cloves
1 cup seeded raisins
1 cup whipping cream for topping

Dissolve soda in combined grated potatoes and

carrots. Stir in melted butter and sugar. Sift flour with salt and spices and add to previous mixture. Stir in raisins. Steam 3 hours in tightly covered, greased pudding mold. Serve hot with the whipped cream, sweetened to taste. Serves 6 to 8.

This economical pudding is dark and rich, quite good enough for Thanksgiving or Christmas dinner.

STEAMING HINTS:

Small round cans with tight-fitting covers may be used to steam puddings in if you have no pudding mold. The top half of a double boiler may also be used, but I've never liked this method as well. Pudding molds must be well greased and covered. Heavy waxed paper held in place with a rubber band will serve as a cover in a pinch.

Fill molds about ⅔ full of batter. Place mold on a trivet in boiling water sufficient to come about halfway up on mold. Old-time cooks used a small wooden rack as a trivet, or even two flat pieces of wood. If the mold shows an inclination to float, place a weight on it.

If water level drops, add more boiling water, but do not allow water to stop boiling.

Old-Fashioned Steamed Pork Pudding

⅔ cup ground fat salt pork (about ½ pound)
⅔ cup light molasses
1 cup sour milk
½ cup sugar
2 cups flour
1 teaspoon baking soda
½ teaspoon cinnamon
½ teaspoon ground cloves
½ teaspoon nutmeg
1 cup chopped seeded raisins
1 cup whipping cream for topping

Add sour milk and molasses to ground salt pork, then stir in the sugar. Sift flour with the baking soda and spices and add to previous mixture with the raisins. Mix well, then pour into greased pudding mold. Steam about 3 hours (*see* Steaming Hints). Serve hot with whipped cream, sweetened to taste. Serves 8.

Pie Pastry for 2 Crusts

2 cups flour
1 teaspoon salt
⅔ cup lard
about ⅓ cup very cold water

Sift flour with the salt and rub in the lard, using knife, pastry blender or fingertips. (If using the latter, as I prefer to do, work swiftly so that the warmth of the fingers will not soften the lard.) Mixture should have a coarse, mealy appearance when lard has been properly rubbed in. Moisten lightly with the cold water, using just barely enough to hold dough together. Do not overmix, but gather together lightly into a ball.

Divide in two equal parts. Place one portion on floured board and roll out about ⅛ inch thick, making pastry about 1 inch larger all around than the pie plate you are to use. Fold in center and place on pie plate, then unfold and fit pastry to plate, trimming edges with a sharp knife.

After pouring in the pie filling, roll out remaining portion of dough in the same manner as before, fitting crust carefully over filling, trimming edges to leave about 1 inch extra on all sides, which should be folded under the edge of bottom crust and pressed firmly to seal. A fork may be used to press edges and to prick center of top crust several times to allow steam to escape.

If a glazed brown top is desired, brush crust with cold milk or water just before putting in oven. Makes 2 crusts for a 9-inch pie.

NOTE: I prefer lard to any other fat for pie pastry, though regular brands of solid shortening are also good. I have never achieved with oil the result I like best.

Pie Pastry for 1 Crust

    1 cup flour
    ½ teaspoon salt
    ⅓ cup lard
    about 3 tablespoons very cold water

Proceed as for pastry for 2-crust pie but do not

divide pastry before rolling. Roll out to about
⅛ inch thick and 1½ inches larger all around
than pie plate. Fold and place in the plate and
fit carefully, taking care not to stretch pastry.
Fold overlapping edge under and flute with
fingers to make a standing rim around edge of
plate. Fill and bake. Makes crust for 9-inch pie.

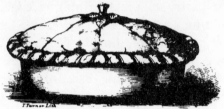

Baked Pie Shell

Make Pie Pastry for 1 Crust, and proceed by the
same method. Be careful not to stretch pastry
when placing it in the pie plate, or it will shrink
back during baking. Flute the standing edge—
also taking care not to press pastry against the
rim of the pie plate (lest the fluting break if you
want to remove the baked shell from the plate
before serving). Prick all around sides and bottom of raw pastry with a fork, to prevent bulges.
Bake about 15 minutes in a 450 oven. Cool before filling. Makes 9-inch shell.

Using Leftover Pie Pastry

Any leftover bits of raw pastry may be made into
small turnovers with a filling of jam.

Or make cinnamon rolls for the children by
spreading rolled-out pastry with a little soft
butter and a mixture of cinnamon and sugar.

Roll up as for jelly roll, slice crosswise in rounds, and bake.

Another special treat for children are jelly tarts made by cutting half the rolled-out pastry with a biscuit cutter, the other half with a doughnut cutter, and pressing the open circle firmly on the round. After baking, put 1 teaspoon of any jelly in the small crater.

Apple-Pumpkin Pie

Pie Pastry for 1 Crust
½ cup light cream
¼ cup milk
1 cup cooked mashed pumpkin
1 cup applesauce, sweetened to taste
½ cup light brown sugar
½ teaspoon salt
1½ teaspoons cinnamon
1½ teaspoons nutmeg
¼ teaspoon ginger
4 eggs, well beaten
¾ cup whipping cream for topping (optional)

Mix milk with cream and scald. Mix pumpkin, applesauce, sugar, salt and spices and add to scalded milk. Stir in beaten eggs and beat well. Pour into pie plate lined with pastry. Bake in 350 oven until silver knife blade comes out clean when inserted in center, or about 40 minutes. Serves 6 to 8.

When serving, a tablespoonful of whipped cream, sweetened to taste, may be put on each piece. A wedge of good store cheese is the perfect accompaniment for this pie.

Sour-Cream Pie

Pie Pastry for 1 Crust
2 eggs, beaten
1 cup sugar
1 tablespoon flour
pinch of salt
1 cup thick sour cream
2 cups chopped seeded raisins

Beat eggs, and add sugar which has been mixed with flour and salt. Add sour cream and beat well. Stir in raisins and pour into a pie plate lined with pastry. Bake in 425 oven for 10 minutes. Reduce heat to 350 and continue baking until filling is set, about 25 minutes longer. Serves 6 to 8.

Buttermilk Pie

1 Baked Pie Shell
2 eggs
2 cups buttermilk
4 teaspoons lemon juice
1 cup sugar
4 tablespoons flour
pinch of salt
¼ cup sugar for meringue

Separate eggs. Beat yolks and add buttermilk and lemon juice. Mix sugar with salt and flour and add to previous mixture. Cook over hot water until thick, stirring constantly. Pour into baked pie shell and cover with meringue made of the 2 egg whites stiffly beaten with the ¼ cup sugar. Brown in 350 oven for about 10 to 12 minutes. Serves 6 to 8.

Mock Cherry (Cranberry) Pie

Pie Pastry for 2 Crusts
3 cups fresh cranberries
1 cup seeded raisins
1¼ cups sugar
2 tablespoons flour
pinch of salt
¾ cup water
½ teaspoon vanilla

Chop cranberries in wooden bowl or put through coarse knife of food grinder. Add raisins, sugar, flour and salt. Stir in the water. Line pie plate with rolled-out pastry and fill with cranberry mixture. Cover with top crust, prick with fork, and bake in 450 oven for 10 minutes. Reduce heat to 350 and continue baking for about 30 minutes more. Serves 6 to 8.

Mock Mince Pie No. 1

Pie Pastry for 2 Crusts
4 tart apples, peeled and chopped (2 cups)
1 cup seeded raisins
1 cup light brown sugar
⅛ teaspoon salt
⅛ teaspoon cinnamon
⅛ teaspoon nutmeg
1 cup sour cream

Add apples to raisins, then stir in sugar, salt, spices and sour cream. Pour into a pie plate lined with pastry, cover with top crust, prick, and bake in 450 oven for 10 minutes. Reduce heat to 350 and continue baking for about 45 minutes. Serve hot with a generous wedge of store cheese.

Mock Mince Pie No. 2

double batch Pie Pastry for 2 Crusts
3 round Common crackers
1 cup hot water
1 cup light molasses
½ cup vinegar
2 eggs, well beaten
½ cup butter, melted
1 cup sugar
¼ teaspoon cinnamon
¼ teaspoon ground cloves
¼ teaspoon nutmeg
¼ teaspoon salt
1 cup chopped seeded raisins

Roll crackers into coarse crumbs. Add hot water, molasses, vinegar, beaten eggs and butter. Mix sugar with spices and salt and add to previous mixture. Stir in chopped raisins. Line two pie plates with pastry and pour ½ the filling in each. Cover with top crusts, prick, and bake in a 450 oven for 10 minutes. Reduce heat to 350 and continue baking for 40 minutes more. This rule may be halved for one pie if desired.

Both Mock Mince Pies are very good, but I

think No. 1 is a little the better. Certainly both are well able to be served on their own merits and not as stand-ins for real mince pie.

Store cheese is almost a must with these!

Salt Pork Apple Pie

Pie Pastry for 2 Crusts
2 ¼-inch slices fat salt pork, diced
6 large tart apples, peeled
1 cup sugar
pinch of cinnamon
pinch of nutmeg

Fry diced salt pork slowly until golden brown, being careful not to burn. Line pie plate with pastry, slice apples and place on crust. Mix sugar with the spices and sprinkle over apples. Pour salt pork with its fat over apples; cover with top crust and prick it. Bake 10 minutes in 425 oven, reduce heat to 350 and continue baking for about 30 minutes more.

Store cheese should be served with this old-fashioned pie.

Mock Apple Pie

Pie Pastry for 2 Crusts
13 saltine crackers
1½ cups hot water
2 tablespoons lemon juice
1 tablespoon butter
1½ cups sugar
1½ teaspoons cream of tartar
½ teaspoon cinnamon
1 teaspoon nutmeg

Break saltines in quarters; add to them the hot water, lemon juice and butter. Mix sugar with cream of tartar and spices and add to previous mixture. Pour into pie plate, which has been lined with pastry. Cover with top crust, prick it, and bake in 400 oven for about 35 minutes.

Strange as it may sound, this rule makes a very good pie, difficult to tell at first taste from apple. This pie may still be found served at church suppers in the deep hill country, where it is quite popular.

Old-Fashioned Green Tomato Pie

Pie Pastry for 2 Crusts
3 cups sliced green tomatoes (about 5 medium)
1⅓ cups sugar
3 tablespoons flour
¼ teaspoon salt
6 tablespoons lemon juice
4 teaspoons grated lemon rind
3 tablespoons butter

Combine sliced green tomatoes with the sugar, salt and flour, then add lemon juice and rind. Pour into pie plate, which has been lined with pastry. Dot with butter, and cover with top crust and prick. Bake in 450 oven for 10 minutes, reduce heat to 350 and continue baking for about 30 minutes more.

Grandmother's Vinegar Pie

1 Baked Pie Shell
2 eggs
½ cup sugar
2 tablespoons butter
3 tablespoons flour
1 teaspoon cinnamon
¼ teaspoon ground cloves
¼ teaspoon allspice
pinch of salt
2 tablespoons vinegar
1 cup water
¼ cup sugar for meringue

Separate eggs and beat yolks. Cream butter and sugar, then beat in egg yolks. Mix flour with spices and salt and add to previous mixture with the water and vinegar. Cook over hot water until thick, stirring constantly. Pour into baked pie shell and top with meringue, which has been made with the egg whites stiffly beaten with the ¼ cup sugar. Brown in 325 oven for 15 minutes.

Best-Ever Pie

Pie Pastry for 1 Crust
2 eggs
1 cup sugar
1 teaspoon cinnamon
½ teaspoon ground cloves
½ cup chopped nutmeats
½ cup seeded raisins
1 tablespoon butter, melted
1 tablespoon vinegar
¾ cup whipping cream for topping

Separate eggs and beat yolks well. Sift sugar with spices and add gradually to egg yolks. Add chopped nuts, raisins and melted butter. Beat egg whites stiff and fold in, adding the vinegar slowly at the same time. Pour into pie plate lined with pastry, bake in 450 oven for 10 minutes, then reduce heat to 350 and bake another 25 mintues. Top should be nicely brown and crisp.

Serve when cool with unsweetened whipped cream. This is truly a party dessert, sweet and very rich.

Carrot Custard Pie

Pie Pastry for 1 Crust
1 cup cooked carrots, mashed very fine
½ teaspoon ginger
¼ teaspoon cinnamon
¼ teaspoon salt
1 cup sugar
1 egg, beaten
1 cup milk, scalded

Add spices, salt and sugar to mashed carrots. Stir in beaten egg, then add the scalded milk. Pour into pie plate, which has been lined with pastry.

Bake in 450 oven for 10 minutes, reduce heat to
350 and continue baking for 25 minutes more, or
until silver knife blade comes out clean when
inserted in middle of pie.

This excellent pie could easily be mistaken for
one made with pumpkin or squash.

Vermont Boiled Cider Pie

Pie Pastry for 2 Crusts
1 egg, beaten
1 cup sugar
⅓ cup flour
½ cup bottled boiled cider
1 cup boiling water

Mix sugar with flour and add to beaten egg. Stir
in the boiled cider, then add the boiling water.
Pour into pie plate which has been lined with
pastry. Roll out top crust, cut into 1-inch strips
and make lattice top (for scraps, *see* Using Leftover Pie Pastry). Bake in 450 oven for 10 minutes, reduce heat and continue baking for about
30 minutes longer.

Boiled cider has become a very scarce com-
modity, yet when I was a girl at home, every
farm was well supplied with this rich reddish-
brown syrup, boiled down each Fall to use for
apple butter, boiled cider applesauce and for
boiled cider pies. A diligent search may be necessary to track down the commercial product,
either in a shop specializing in Vermont products or in a deep-hill-country grocery store. But
it is gettable.

Poor Man's Lemon Pie

1 Baked Pie Shell
2 eggs
1¼ cups sugar
3 tablespoons cornstarch
1 teaspoon cream of tartar
2 teaspoons lemon extract
2 cups hot water
1 tablespoon butter
¼ cup sugar for meringue

Separate eggs and beat yolks well, blending in the sugar. Mix cornstarch with the cream of tartar and add to first mixture. Stir in lemon extract slowly, then add slowly the hot water in which the butter has been melted. Cool, then pour into baked pie shell and top with meringue made with the egg whites stiffly beaten with the ¼ cup sugar. Brown in 325 oven for about 15 minutes.

This recipe makes a very good lemon pie, although it's not quite so tart as one made in the orthodox way.

CHAPTER NINE

Maple Sugar and
Maple Syrup

A LARGE PROPORTION of the recipes handed down in New England's hill country have maple sugar or maple syrup as an ingredient, and range from baked beans to cakes, puddings and pies, and include breads of all kinds. Some of these rules are unique, and all are evidence of the inspiration and ingenuity of housewives who knew how to use the golden-brown sweetening to the best advantage.

Maple sugar and maple syrup weren't considered delicacies: they were a commonplace article of food, like any other product of the farm, and the superb flavor that maple imparts to all things made with it was taken for granted.

Its versatility meant that it appeared at almost every meal, however informal. On baking day, it was routine to pinch off part of the white-bread dough to make into maple-butternut rolls

—which were simply a little crushed maple sugar and butternuts in the bottom of buttered muffin cups and covered with a ball of dough, then set aside to rise and be baked as usual. Or apples were brought from down cellar, cored and filled with maple sugar and baked on a pie plate, to be eaten with a spoonful of yellow cream. On Winter evenings, Common crackers were split, each half buttered, sprinkled with maple sugar and moistened with cream, then popped into the oven for a few minutes to emerge puffed high, brown and sweet.

And whenever he felt in the mood, any member of the family was at liberty to gouge a lump of sugar from the firkin in the pantry, either to nibble or to crumble on a slice of well-buttered bread.

NOTE: More about maple itself is in *Translations* in the front of this book; more rules for using it in Chapter Ten, *Candy,* and Vermont Baked Beans and Maple Candied Sweet Potatoes are included in *Vegetables.*

Maple Brown Bread

      1 cup cornmeal
      1¾ cups graham flour
      1 teaspoon salt
      1 teaspoon baking soda
      1 cup maple syrup
      2 cups buttermilk (or sour milk)
      1 cup seeded raisins (optional)

Add cornmeal to graham flour, mixing in salt and baking soda, but do not sift. Add maple syrup to buttermilk and stir into previous mixture. Add raisins if desired. Mix thoroughly and pour into large greased mold, about 1½ quarts capacity. Batter should not fill mold more than ⅔ full. Cover and steam about 3 hours (*see* Steaming Hints). If preferred, this brown bread may be baked in 2 small greased bread tins, about 4 x 8, in a 325 oven for about 1 hour.

Maple Bran Bread

1½ cups flour
3½ teaspoons any baking powder
1 teaspoon salt
3 tablespoons sugar
1 cup bran
½ cup chopped dates
1 egg
⅔ cup warm milk
½ cup maple syrup
½ cup butter, melted

Sift flour with baking powder, sugar and salt. Mix in bran and dates. Beat egg into milk and maple syrup; add melted butter, then stir into flour mixture. Don't mix too much, just enough

to wet ingredients well. Bake in greased standard
bread tin for about 1 hour in 350 oven.

Maple Coffee Cake

1½ cups sifted flour
½ cup whole-wheat flour
4 teaspoons any baking powder
1 teaspoon salt
¼ teaspoon cinnamon
pinch of nutmeg
2 tablespoons butter, melted
1 egg, well beaten
⅔ cup maple syrup
⅔ cup milk
1 teaspoon cinnamon for topping (optional)
2 tablespoons sugar for topping (optional)

Sift dry ingredients together. Mix maple syrup,
milk, egg and melted butter and stir into first
mixture. Mix only enough to wet ingredients
thoroughly—do not beat. Pour into greased
square cake pan, about 9½ x 9½, and sprinkle
top with the cinnamon-and-sugar mixture if desired. Bake about 30 minutes in 400 oven. Serves
6 to 8.

Maple Oatmeal Bread

2 cups rolled oats
2 cups boiling water
1 tablespoon lard
½ cup maple syrup
1½ teaspoons salt
1 yeast cake (or envelope)
½ cup lukewarm water
about 5 cups flour

Pour the boiling water over rolled oats, add lard, maple syrup and the salt. Let stand until lukewarm, then add yeast which has been dissolved in the lukewarm water. Add flour, making a stiff dough (if necessary a little more flour may be added). Turn out on floured board and knead well. Place in large bowl, cover and let rise in a warm place until doubled in bulk. Knead down again on floured board until dough is smooth and elastic. Divide into 2 parts and shape into loaves. Place in greased standard bread tins, cover with a towel and let rise until doubled. Bake in 375 oven for about 1 hour. Makes 2 loaves.

Maple Syrup Gingerbread

1 cup maple syrup
1 cup sour cream
1 egg, beaten
2⅓ cups flour
1¼ teaspoons baking soda
½ teaspoon salt
1½ teaspoons ground ginger
4 tablespoons shortening, melted (or oil)
¾ cup whipping cream for topping (optional)

Mix maple syrup and sour cream with the beaten egg. Sift flour with the soda, salt and ginger and add to first mixture. Mix well, then add melted shortening. Beat all thoroughly. Pour into greased cake pan, about 9 x 9, and bake in 375 oven for about 35 minutes. Serve warm with whipped cream, sweetened to taste, if desired. Serves 6 to 8.

Maple Layer Biscuits

2 cups flour
3 teaspoons any baking powder
½ teaspoon salt
4 tablespoons shortening
¾ cup milk
½ cup crushed maple sugar (good ¼ pound)

Sift flour, salt and baking powder together, rub shortening in with fingers. Add milk. Mix lightly and turn out on floured board. Knead very slightly into a smooth dough, roll out to about ½ inch thick. Sprinkle dough with finely crushed maple sugar. Fold dough over twice and roll out again to about ¾ inch thick. Cut with round biscuit cutter and place in greased baking pan. Bake in 450 oven for about 15 minutes. Makes about 15 biscuits.

Apple Roll

1 batch Buttermilk Biscuit dough
1⅓ cups maple syrup
1⅓ cups water
1 tablespoon butter
3 tart medium apples, peeled

Bring maple syrup, water and the butter to the boiling point and simmer 5 minutes, then pour into a buttered baking dish, about 8 x 10 x 2. Roll biscuit dough to about ½ inch thick. Slice apples in thin slices (about ¼-inch) and arrange on dough. Roll up like a jelly roll and cut crosswise in 1½-inch slices. Place cut-side-down in syrup in the baking pan, and bake in 400 oven until brown, about 15 to 18 minutes. Spoon warm sauce from the pan over each serving, with either whipped or plain cream. Serves 8.

Rich Maple Shortcake

> 2 cups flour
> 1 tablespoon baking powder
> ¼ teaspoon salt
> ½ cup softened butter
> about ¾ cup milk
> about 2½ cups Maple Filling

Sift flour with baking powder and salt, then rub in butter with the fingers. Add the milk to make a soft dough. Turn out on floured board and divide dough in 2 equal parts. Grease 2 8-inch pie plates and roll out each portion of dough to fit its plate. Bake in 400 oven until golden brown, about 18 minutes. Spread Maple Filling between layers and over top. Serves 8.

This is another very old recipe and is quite delicious, although very sweet and rich.

MAPLE FILLING:

> ¾ cup maple syrup
> 1 tablespoon butter
> 2 egg whites, beaten stiff
> ½ cup cream, beaten stiff
> ½ teaspoon vanilla

Boil maple syrup and butter until it will spin a thread, or to 238 degrees. Pour hot syrup on very stiffly beaten egg whites very slowly, beating constantly. Continue beating until filling is thick and smooth. Fold in stiffly beaten cream and flavor with the vanilla.

Maple Syrup Layer Cake

½ cup soft butter
1 cup white sugar less 1 tablespoon
2 large eggs, beaten
2¾ cups sifted flour
2½ teaspoons baking powder
1 teaspoon salt
½ cup milk
1 cup maple syrup
about 2 cups Maple Syrup Frosting
½ cup walnut halves for top

Cream butter and sugar until light, then beat in eggs. Sift flour with baking powder and salt. Add milk to maple syrup. Add flour mixture to egg mixture alternately with syrup mixture, beating very smooth after each addition. Pour into 2 greased layer-cake pans and bake about 30 minutes in 350 oven. Cool and put layers together with Maple Syrup Frosting, spreading it over top and sides. Decorate top of cake with walnut halves.

MAPLE SYRUP FROSTING:

1¼ cups maple syrup
2 egg whites, stiffly beaten

Boil maple syrup until it makes a firm ball when tested in cold water, or to about 250 degrees. Beat very gradually into the stiffly beaten egg whites. Continue beating until frosting holds its shape. Makes about 2 cups.

Maple Upsidedown Cake

1 tablespoon soft butter
3 tablespoons white sugar
1 egg, beaten
1 cup flour
2 teaspoons any baking powder
pinch of salt
½ cup milk
1 cup maple syrup

Cream butter with the sugar, then beat in egg. Sift flour with baking powder and salt and add to first mixture, with the milk. Beat all very well. Bring maple syrup to boiling point and pour into bottom of buttered baking dish, about 9 x 9. Pour batter in on top of syrup. Bake in 400 oven for about 30 minutes. Turn out upsidedown on a platter. Serve warm with plain or whipped cream. Will serve 6 to 8.

Maple Syrup Sponge Cake

¾ cup maple syrup
4 eggs
1 cup sifted flour
1 teaspoon any baking powder
¼ teaspoon salt
½ teaspoon vanilla

Bring maple syrup to the boiling point. Separate eggs, beat whites very stiff and pour onto them, very slowly, the hot maple syrup, continuing to beat. Beat egg yolks until light and add to syrup mixture. Sift dry ingredients together 3 times, then fold into previous mixture. Dust an ungreased tube cake pan with flour. Pour in batter and bake in 325 oven for about 50 minutes. Invert pan and let cake cool before removing.

Maple Sugar Bars

¼ cup butter, softened
1 cup crushed maple sugar (good ½ pound)
1 egg, beaten
1 cup flour
1 teaspoon any baking powder
¼ teaspoon salt
1 cup broken nutmeats
½ teaspoon vanilla

Cream maple sugar with softened butter and beat in the egg. Sift flour with baking powder and salt, then add nutmeats. Add flour mixture to egg mixture. Add vanilla. Blend well and pour into greased square cake pan, about 8 x 8, and bake in 350 oven for about 25 minutes. Cut in squares. Makes 16.

These are similar to butterscotch squares, brown and chewy but delightfully maple-y in flavor.

Sour-Cream Maple Spice Cookies

    1 cup seedless raisins
    hot water
    1 cup sour cream
    1 teaspoon baking soda
    1 cup light molasses
    1 cup crushed maple sugar (good ½ pound)
    2 eggs, well beaten
    4 cups flour
    1 teaspoon cinnamon
    1 teaspoon ground cloves
    ½ teaspoon salt

Cover raisins with hot water and let stand a few minutes to plump up. Meanwhile add the soda to the sour cream, then add molasses and maple sugar. Add beaten eggs. Sift flour with spices and the salt and add to previous mixture. Drain raisins well and add. Drop from teaspoon on greased cookie sheet, and bake in 400 oven for about 15 minutes. Makes about 5 dozen.

Old-Fashioned Indian Pudding

    5 tablespoons yellow cornmeal
    4 cups milk, scalded
    2 tablespoons butter
    1 cup maple syrup
    2 eggs, beaten
    1 teaspoon cinnamon
    ¾ teaspoon ginger
    1 teaspoon salt
    1 cup cold milk

Add cornmeal to hot milk, stirring constantly. Cook over low heat until thickened, stirring constantly. Remove from heat, add butter, maple syrup, beaten eggs, spices and salt. Mix well and pour into buttered baking dish. Bake in 300 oven for about 1 hour. Stir and add the 1 cup of cold milk and continue baking for 1 more hour. Serve warm with plain or whipped cream. Serves 8 to 10.

Maple Bread Pudding

2 cups stale breadcrumbs
4 cups milk, scalded
¾ cup maple syrup
¼ cup butter, melted
2 eggs, slightly beaten
½ teaspoon salt
½ cup broken butternut meats

Pour hot milk over the breadcrumbs and cool. Add maple syrup, melted butter and the slightly beaten eggs. Add salt and butternuts. Stir to mix, then pour into buttered baking dish. Bake in 325 oven for about 1 hour. Serve with plain or whipped cream. Walnuts may be used instead of butternuts. Serves 6 to 8.

Steamed Maple Chocolate Pudding

2 cups sifted flour
4½ teaspoons baking powder
¼ teaspoon salt
1 cup maple syrup
½ cup water
½ cup hot mashed potato (about 1 large)
1 egg, beaten
2½ ounces baking chocolate
3 tablespoons butter
1 cup whipping cream for topping

Sift flour, baking powder and salt together. Mix maple syrup with the water and stir into flour mixture. Add mashed potato and beaten egg, beating in well. Add chocolate and butter, which have been melted over hot water, beating all well. Turn into greased mold of about 1 quart capacity, cover tightly and steam about 3 hours (*see* Steaming Hints). Serve warm with whipped cream, sweetened to taste. Serves 8.

Maple Charlotte Russe

1 tablespoon gelatine
¼ cup cold water
¾ cup maple syrup
2 cups whipping cream
½ teaspoon vanilla

Soak gelatine in cold water for about 5 minutes. Bring maple syrup to the boiling point. Dissolve the gelatine in the hot syrup, then set aside to cool. Before it begins to stiffen, beat cream until stiff and fold in. Add vanilla. Pour into mold and harden in refrigerator. Serves 6 to 8.

Maple Mousse

3 egg yolks
1 cup maple syrup
4 cups whipping cream
½ teaspoon vanilla

Heat maple syrup until just below boiling point. Beat egg yolks until light, then add hot syrup gradually, stirring constantly. Set aside to cool. Whip cream stiff and fold into cooled egg-and-syrup mixture. Add vanilla. Pour into 1-gallon can that has a lid. Cover tightly and pack can in ice and rock salt to cover. Let stand 3 hours. Makes about 2 quarts.

A hand ice-cream freezer is good for this purpose because the dasher can be removed and the hole at the top covered to keep out any salt or water. This mousse can also be frozen in the ice-cube trays in the freezing compartment of your refrigerator and will be quite as creamy.

If necessary, the mousse can be placed in a covered metal can in the deep freeze, but you will need to take it out well in advance of serving time, or it will be too hard to serve.

Maple-Nut Tapioca Pudding

2 cups milk
¼ cup Minute tapioca
⅔ cup maple syrup
½ teaspoon salt
1 egg
½ cup chopped nutmeats
½ cup whipping cream for topping

Mix milk, tapioca, salt and maple syrup together. Cook over hot water for 15 minutes, stirring frequently. Separate the egg, beating the yolk well. Stir a few spoonfuls of the hot milk mixture into the beaten yolk, stirring to prevent curdling. Add rest of hot mixture, and stir for 3 minutes over hot water. Cool, add nutmeats, then fold in stiffly beaten egg white. Pour into bowl and cool, then refrigerate until served. Whip cream, sweeten to taste and top each serving. Serves 6.

This is a soft, creamy pudding, well flavored with maple.

Old-Fashioned Maple Sugar Pie

Pie Pastry for 2 Crusts
1 cup crushed maple sugar (good ½ pound)
1 tablespoon flour
⅛ teaspoon nutmeg
pinch of salt
2 eggs, beaten
½ cup cream

Mix crushed maple sugar with flour, nutmeg and salt. Beat eggs well and add the sugar mixture. Add cream. Pour mixture into pie plate lined with pastry; cover with top crust, prick. Bake in 450 oven for 10 minutes. Reduce heat to 350 and continue baking for about 25 . minutes longer.

This is a very old recipe from the days when people knew nothing about calories! It is quite sweet and rich, the interior the consistency of a dark golden custard. Serve in quite small wedges since it is a heavy dessert. I've found that store cheese goes very well with this pie, its tang a welcome complement to the sweetness.

Maple-Nut Pie

1 Baked Pie Shell
1½ tablespoons butter, melted
2 tablespoons flour
2 eggs
1 cup maple syrup
⅓ cup water
¾ cup broken butternut meats
¼ cup sugar for meringue

Melt butter and stir in the flour. Separate eggs; beat the yolks, add the maple syrup and water and blend all into the butter-and-flour paste. Cook over hot water until thick, stirring constantly. Add butternuts and pour into baked pie shell. Top with meringue made from egg whites beaten stiff with the ¼ cup sugar. Brown in 325 oven for about 15 minutes.

Maple Cream Pie

1 Baked Pie Shell
⅔ cup crushed maple sugar (good ⅓ pound)
2 tablespoons cornstarch
¼ teaspoon salt
2 eggs
2 cups milk
½ teaspoon vanilla
¼ cup sugar for meringue

Mix maple sugar with cornstarch and salt. Separate eggs; beat yolks and blend thoroughly with sugar mixture. Add milk. Cook over hot water until thickened, stirring constantly. Remove from heat and add vanilla. Pour into baked pie shell and top with meringue made from the egg whites beaten stiff with the ¼ cup sugar. Brown in 325 oven for 15 minutes.

Apple Dumplings

Pie Pastry for 2 Crusts
6 medium apples, firm and tart
½ cup crushed maple sugar (good ¼ pound)
½ cup white sugar
1 teaspoon cinnamon
pinch of salt
¼ teaspoon nutmeg
½ cup apple jelly
1½ tablespoons butter

Peel and core apples. Mix the sugars with cinnamon, salt and nutmeg, stir in the apple jelly. Fill cavities in the apples with equal amounts of the sugar-and-jelly mixture. Dot with the butter. Roll pie pastry about ¼ inch thick and cut in 6 squares, each large enough to wrap an apple. Place apple on pastry square and pinch pastry together at the top. Bake in greased baking pan in 450 oven for 10 minutes. Reduce heat to 350 and bake about 30 minutes more, or until apples are tender and crust is brown. Serve warm with cream. Serves 6.

Peaches Baked in Maple Syrup

6 large fresh peaches
¾ cup maple syrup

Peel and halve peaches, removing pit. Place cut-side-down in buttered baking dish. Add syrup. Bake in 350 oven for about 20 to 25 minutes, spooning syrup up over peaches occasionally. Serve warm or cold, with whipped or plain cream.

Maple Apples

2 cups maple syrup
2 cups water
6 large apples, firm and tart

Boil syrup and water together for 10 minutes. Peel and core apples and simmer whole in the syrup until tender, turning carefully with a fork once or twice. Serve warm with a spoonful of the syrup, and with cream if desired.

CHAPTER TEN

Candy

THE ONLY candy-making equipment my mother had was a blue agate saucepan, a long wooden spoon and a cup of cold water. Yet her products, cooked over a wood fire and using only the ingredients found on the farm, were as delicious as any found in big-city stores today.

I've often thought that the good Lord caused maple and butternut trees to grow side by side on New England hillsides because of the natural and wonderful affinity the product of the one tree has for that of the other. Maple sugar and butternuts belong together, a fact never more evident than in maple butternut fudge, satin smooth and the color of a lightly creamed cup of coffee.

Candy had an important place in the scheme of things on yesterday's hill farms, and the best of it was made at home from materials that cost nothing. The root of the sweet flag that grew in the marshy spots of the meadows was delicious when candied. There was an infinite variety of maple fudges, creams and brittles to be made; pungent peppermint drops that old-time people valued for their soothing effect on the stomach, and dried horehound from the garden found its way into glistening brown horehound candies to ease a sore throat or cough. And many a courtship began at taffy pulls, those high spots in the social calendar of every neighborhood.

Maple Syrup Butternut Fudge

    2 cups white sugar
    1 cup maple syrup
    1 tablespoon light corn syrup
    1 cup milk
    1 tablespoon butter
    1 cup broken butternut meats

Cook sugar, syrup, milk and butter together until it forms a soft ball in cold water, about 238 degrees. Cool, beat until creamy and thick, add nuts and pour at once into buttered pan. Mark into squares. Makes about 1½ pounds.

Maple Divinity

    2 cups maple syrup
    2 cups white sugar
    2 egg whites, beaten stiff
    2 cups broken butternut neats

Boil sugar and water until it spins a 3-inch

thread, 238 degrees. Pour very slowly over stiffly beaten egg whites, beating constantly. Continue beating until candy will hold its shape. Add nuts, pour at once into buttered pan and mark into squares. Walnuts may be used instead of butternuts. Makes about 1¾ pounds.

Maple Caramels

    2 cups light brown sugar
    1½ cups maple syrup
    ½ cup cream
    1 tablespoon butter

Mix sugar, maple syrup and cream. Stir over quick heat until sugar is melted. Reduce heat and stir until mixture makes a soft ball when tested in cold water, 238 degrees. Add the butter and pour at once into buttered shallow pan. Just before the candy hardens, cut into squares. Makes about 1½ pounds.

Quick Maple Creams

    4 cups maple syrup
    1 cup cream
    ¼ cup butter
    1 cup broken nutmeats
    1 teaspoon lemon extract

Bring maple syrup, butter and cream to a full boil and cook for exactly 9 minutes after mixture begins to boil. Remove from heat, add nuts and lemon extract. Stir for exactly 5 minutes, then pour at once into buttered shallow pan. Cut into squares when cool. This candy has a creamy texture and is a true maple cream recipe. Makes about 2 pounds.

Maple Chocolate Fudge

1 cup crushed maple sugar (good ½ pound)
1 cup light brown sugar
2 tablespoons butter
¾ cup light corn syrup
2 ounces bitter baking chocolate
¾ cup cream
1 cup broken nutmeats

Mix all ingredients except nuts and cook over low heat, stirring constantly, until candy makes a soft ball when tested in cold water, or 238 degrees. Remove from heat and beat until smooth and creamy. Add nuts and pour at once into buttered shallow pan. Mark into squares when cool. Makes about 1½ pounds.

Maple Popcorn Balls

1¾ cups corn, popped (3½ quarts)
1 teaspoon salt
1¼ cups white sugar
1¼ cups crushed maple sugar (5/8 pound)
½ cup light corn syrup
⅔ cup water
1 tablespoon butter
1 cup broken nutmeats (optional)

Put popped corn in large bowl and sprinkle with the 1 teaspoon salt. Mix sugars with the syrup and the water and cook over low heat until sugar is dissolved, stirring constantly. Add butter and continue cooking without stirring until mixture forms a soft ball when tested in cold water, 238 degrees. Remove from fire and pour over the popped corn, mixing thoroughly. When cool enough to handle comfortably, form into balls about 2½ inches in diameter, greasing hands well before handling corn. Place balls on waxed paper to harden outside coating. Extra-special balls may be made by adding broken nutmeats just before shaping. Makes about 15 balls.

Maple Molasses Chews

4 cups light molasses
1 cup light brown sugar
1 cup crushed maple sugar (good ½ pound)
pinch of cream of tartar
½ cup butter
½ teaspoon vinegar
pinch of salt
1 teaspoon vanilla
2 cups broken nutmeats

Cook molasses, sugars and cream of tartar until mixture forms a hard ball when tested in cold water, 270 degrees. Remove from fire and add butter, vinegar, salt, vanilla and nuts, stirring just enough to blend. Pour into buttered shallow pan and mark into squares while still soft. This chewy molasses candy is well flavored with the maple sugar, making it a little out of the ordinary. Makes about 2½ pounds.

Molasses Mint Taffy

2 cups light molassess
2 teaspoons vinegar
1½ tablespoons butter
pinch of salt
½ teaspoon baking soda
7 drops oil of peppermint

Cook molasses and vinegar over low heat, stirring constantly, until candy is brittle when tested in cold water, 290 to 310 degrees. Remove from heat, add butter, salt and soda. Stir until candy stops foaming, then pour into buttered shallow pan. When cool enough to handle, pour peppermint oil into center of candy and work in, drawing corners toward the center. Hands should be well buttered for pulling candy. Remove from pan and pull until light colored and firm. Pull into long rope and cut in pieces. Wrap each piece in waxed paper. Makes about 1½ pounds.

Old-Fashioned Peppermint Drops

2 cups sugar
½ cup cold water
¼ teaspoon cream of tartar
10 drops oil of peppermint

Cook sugar, cold water and cream of tartar without stirring until candy forms soft ball when tested in cold water, 238 degrees. Remove from heat and let stand 2 minutes. Add oil of peppermint and beat until mixture is creamy and beginning to cool. Drop from teaspoon onto waxed paper to harden. Makes about 1 pound.

These peppermint drops have a creamy consistency and a pronounced peppermint flavor. My great-grandmother always kept a supply of them at hand "as an aid to digestion," which I think was the secret of this candy's popularity with an older generation.

Mexican Orange Candy

3 cups sugar
¼ cup boiling water
1 cup evaporated milk
¼ teaspoon salt
grated rind of 2 oranges
grated rind of ½ lemon
4 tablespoons butter
1 cup broken nutmeats

Place 1 cup of the sugar in a heavy spider and melt over very low heat. Add boiling water and cook until the mixture is a heavy, smooth syrup. Add remaining 2 cups sugar, the evaporated milk and the salt. Continue cooking until candy forms a firm ball when tested in cold water, 250 degrees. Add grated rinds and the butter. Cool slightly, add nuts and beat until smooth and creamy. Pour into shallow buttered pan. Mark into squares when cool. This delicious candy is similar to a fudge but with a quite different flavor. Makes about 1¾ pounds.

This receipt was brought back to Vermont in 1904 by a young bride who went to California with her husband—only to find that the green Yankee hills were what they both wanted after all.

Fluffy Molasses Candy

1 cup light molasses
½ cup sugar
1 tablespoon butter
1 tablespoon vinegar
pinch of salt
1 teaspoon baking soda
½ cup broken nutmeats

Boil molasses, sugar, butter, vinegar and salt until brittle when tested in cold water, 290 to 310 degrees. Remove from heat, add the 1 teaspoon baking soda and beat until well blended. Stir in nutmeats and pour into shallow buttered pan. Mark into squares when cool. Makes about ¾ pound.

This is a hard candy, so the name apparently refers to its fluffy appearance, given by the soda.

Simple Chocolates

> 1 small potato, freshly boiled and mashed
> ¼ teaspoon salt
> about 2½ cups confectioner's sugar
> 1 teaspoon vanilla
> food coloring (optional)
> oil of peppermint (optional)
> lemon extract (optional)
> oil of wintergreen (optional)
> about 1 cup Chocolate Coating

Add salt and vanilla to hot mashed potato. Work in enough confectioner's sugar to make a stiff fondant that will hold its shape when fashioned into small balls with the fingers. Place balls on waxed paper until all are ready to dip. Dip in coating and set on waxed paper to dry. This simply made fondant is creamy and good. Makes about 20 to 24 small balls.

The vanilla may be omitted and the fondant colored green and flavored to taste with the peppermint; or colored pink and flavored with wintergreen, or colored yellow and flavored with the lemon extract. I sometimes like to divide fondant in four parts, leaving one uncolored and using ¼ teaspoon vanilla, and adding assorted colors and flavors to the other three.

CHOCOLATE COATING:

> 2 squares bitter baking chocolate
> 2 squares sweet milk chocolate
> 2 tablespoons butter
> 1 x 1 x ½-inch square of paraffin
> ¼ teaspoon vanilla

Place all ingredients except vanilla in double boiler and stir until melted and blended; add vanilla. Remove from heat and cool, then dip fondant balls. Use a fork and dip quickly, allowing excess chocolate to drip back into pan. Don't try to dip chocolates on a hot or humid day: about 65 degrees temperature is best. Makes about 1 cup.

Apple Crystals

3 cups white sugar
1½ cups water
5 medium firm apples

Cook sugar and water over low heat, stirring until sugar is dissolved. Bring to boiling point. Have apples peeled, cored and quartered. Cut each quarter into 3 slices. Drop 12 slices at a time into the syrup and cook gently until transparent. Add ¼ cup hot water to syrup after each 12 slices are removed, since the syrup cooks down. Repeat until all slices are cooked.

Dry apple slices on waxed paper in cool, dry place for 24 hours. Roll slices in granulated sugar and let dry again for 24 hours. Repeat twice more. After third time, let slices stand until they are so dry no moisture can be seen coming from them. Pack in flat containers and store in cool, dry place.

This amount of syrup will make about 5 dozen slices.

Horehound Candy

1 ounce dried horehound
1½ cups water
4⅓ cups light brown sugar, well packed
¼ cup light corn syrup

Simmer horehound in the water for about 30 minutes, then strain. To the liquid, add the sugar and corn syrup. Cook until brittle when tested in cold water, 290 to 310 degrees. Pour into greased shallow pan and mark into small squares. Makes about 2 pounds.

the pale tawny red of early apple jelly to the dark purple of wild blackberry jam.

In Winter plain meals were made festive with tender, crisp pickles or spiced crabapples. School lunches sprang delightful surprises—wild strawberry jam between slices of homemade bread, or a turnover filled with raspberries that had lost little of their flavor after months in a jar.

LIKE THE long-gone cooks who filled the last pages of their handwritten cookbooks with entries for favorite odds and ends, I can't resist adding a ·rule for that quaint thirst-quencher known as Switchel. And perhaps someone else, too, will enjoy Blackberry Cordial, as potent a drink as it is pleasant.

Notes on Preserving

The rules that follow took a lot for granted, especially the time the housewife was prepared to spend in putting down the harvest and the knowledge she had gained from experience as to amounts and methods—and I've endeavored to fill in their gaps for modern cooks without sacrificing their simplicity. But here are a few random hints, in addition.

JELLING:

Old-time cooks knew little or nothing about pectin—except that some fruit juices would jell satisfactorily and some would not. So when they used fruits that don't jell readily by themselves

—such as peaches or strawberries—they merely added the juice from apples or currants to insure the needed firmness. Fruit skins not only furnished pretty color but also added jelling quality to the juices used.

Jelly Bags:

Cloth bags for straining juices can be made of any closely woven white material (like muslin) that will not let juice run through too rapidly; they can be rigged with a bent wire coat hanger and suspended in any out-of-the-way corner of the kitchen. Squeezing the jelly bag will add to the amount of juice extracted, but will make a cloudy product.

Sheeting Test:

If you have no thermometer, you can test the boiling jelly with a spoon for degree of doneness. Start testing about 5 minutes after adding the sugar. Take a spoonful of the juice, cool for a moment, and pour back into the kettle. The first tests will show 2 drops forming from the side of the spoon. But when the jelly is ready these drops will merge and tear off the spoon in a manner known as "sheeting."

Jars and Glasses:

Glass containers for any type of preserving should be scrubbed and sterilized in hot water, and filled while still hot if possible. Standing the glasses or jars in a few inches of hot water in a wide pan will help prevent breakage when being filled with boiling-hot liquids.

SEALING:

Melted paraffin should be poured over jelly at once. Spoiled jelly often results from allowing the jelly to stand too long before sealing with wax. Provide metal covers for jelly containers: mice like paraffin.

Always melt paraffin slowly and in small amounts at a time (it's flammable, after all). If some wax does catch fire *don't pour water on it —smother the flame with salt.*

All preserving should be sealed at once in tightly capped jars. Buy fresh rubber rings at the start of each canning season for those types of jars requiring them.

Chokecherry Jelly

   1 cup chokecherry juice

   3 cups apple juice

   2⅔ cups sugar

Add the sugar to blended juice and boil until liquid sheets from the spoon, 220 degrees. Skim if a film appears on the surface of boiling mixture. Pour at once into hot sterile glasses to about ¼ inch from the top. Cover with melted paraffin immediately, making about an ⅛-inch seal, and cap with metal covers. Makes 4 to 5 glasses.

Chokecherry juice may be obtained by boiling chokecherries in lidded kettle in water just covering for about 30 minutes, then straining through jelly bag. Apple juice is obtained in the same manner: simmer cut-up unpeeled apples in water barely covering for about 20 minutes (in a covered kettle), then strain through jelly bag.

Spiced Apple Jelly

1 peck tart apples
1 pint vinegar
1 quart water
1½ ounces stick cinnamon
½ ounce whole cloves
about 4 to 5 pounds sugar

Cut up whole apples, add water and vinegar. Tie spices in small cloth bag and add to apples. Boil all together in covered kettle until apples are mushy. Strain through jelly bag, but do not squeeze or jelly will be cloudy.

Measure juice and add sugar, cup for cup. Return to stove and boil until jelly sheets from the spoon, 220 degrees. Skim, pour into hot glasses; seal with paraffin and cap. Makes about 10 glasses.

Apple Marmalade

5 pounds tart apples
2 oranges
2 lemons
5 pounds sugar
2½ cups water

Pare and core apples, then cut in thin slices. Add juice of lemons and oranges, cut peel in thin

strips and add. Make syrup of the sugar and
water. Add to fruit mixture and simmer very
slowly until thick. Pour into hot jars and seal
at once. Makes about 4 pints.

Carrot Marmalade

    4 cups cooked carrots
    2 lemons
    2 oranges
    6½ cups sugar

Put carrots and seeded lemons and oranges
through coarse knife of food grinder. Be,sure to
save all juice. Add sugar and cook very slowly
until thick. Pour into hot jars and seal at once.
Makes about 3 pints.

This marmalade is beautifully colored and of
excellent flavor, and is as much a favorite today
as it was many years ago.

Tomato Preserve

    24 large ripe tomatoes
    about 4 to 5 pounds sugar
    9 ripe peaches, peeled and sliced
    1 tablespoon vanilla

Peel, cut up and measure the tomatoes. To every
4 cups of the tomatoes, use 3 cups sugar. Cook
very slowly in their own juice for about 1 hour.
Add sliced peaches and simmer until thick. Add

vanilla. Seal at once in hot, lidded jars. Makes about 6 pints.

Rhubarb Conserve

5 pounds rhubarb
1 pound seeded raisins
5 pounds sugar
1 lemon
2 oranges

Cut unpeeled rhubarb into 1-inch pieces. Mix with the sugar and let stand overnight. In the morning add finely chopped or ground raisins. Add the juice of the lemon and oranges. Put orange and lemon rinds through food grinder and add to rhubarb mixture. Cook all very slowly until thick. Pour into hot jelly glasses and seal at once with paraffin; or pint Mason jars may be used, sealing while hot. Makes 5 to 6 pints.

Tutti Frutti

1 pint brandy
16 cups fruit or berries
16 scant cups sugar

Place brandy in a stone crock that has a well-fitting cover. Add a total of 16 cups of fruits as they ripen, using the same amount of sugar as fruit. Use only firm, ripe fruit. (You may have to add more brandy if total of fruit additions is more than 4 quarts). Stir mixture every day until last fruit has been added, then cover crock and put away in a cool place.

Because of their natures, citrus fruits make an inferior product, so it is well not to use them. Strawberries, raspberries, cherries, currants, gooseberries and peaches are all good. A fresh pineapple, peeled and cut up, may also be used.

This brandied fruit mixture will keep indefinitely and may be used as a dessert or as a condiment with meats. It was considered a "company" dish in olden times: even the visiting ministers were fond of it and, apparently, never associated it with an alcoholic beverage.

Green Tomato Mincemeat

  4 pounds green tomatoes, chopped
  4 pounds apples, peeled and chopped
  3 oranges
  3 cups chopped seeded raisins
  1 tablespoon salt
  4 pounds light brown sugar (9 cups packed)
  ½ pound chopped suet
  1 cup vinegar
  1 tablespoon cinnamon
  ½ tablespoon nutmeg
  ½ tablespoon ground cloves
  ¼ pound candied peel (optional)

Pour boiling water over chopped tomatoes and drain. Repeat and drain well. Add grated rind of 1 orange and juice of all 3. Add remaining ingredients. Simmer all very slowly until thick and dark. Seal in hot Mason jars.

A richer filling may be made by adding the ¼ pound mixed candied lemon peel, orange peel and citron. This is an excellent mincemeat and many people prefer it to that made with beef. Makes about 5 quarts.

Tomato Fruit Chili Sauce

6 peaches
6 pears
20 ripe medium tomatoes
8 medium onions
3 large sweet red peppers
2¾ cups sugar
3 cups vinegar
1 cup water
5 teaspoons salt
14 whole cloves
6 sticks whole cinnamon

Peel peaches and discard pits. Peel tomatoes, core pears and remove seeds from the peppers. Put all fruit and vegetables through the food grinder. Tie spices in small cloth bag. Dilute vinegar with the water. Mix all ingredients and cook very slowly until thick. Remove cloth bag of spices, pour into hot Mason jars, and seal at once. Makes about 5 quarts.

Pickled Crabapples

8 pounds crabapples
6 cups vinegar
8 cups light brown sugar
2 teaspoons whole cloves
2 cinnamon sticks

Cut out blossom end of crabapple, leave stem on and pierce fruit several times with a large

needle. Mix vinegar with the sugar, tie spices in
a small cloth bag and simmer about 5 minutes
together to make syrup. Simmer fruit in the
syrup until tender but not mushy, about 10 minutes. Remove spice bag and pack fruit in hot
glass jars, pouring hot syrup over to fill each
container. Seal at once. Makes about 4 quarts.

Pickled Prunes

> 1 pound large prunes
> 1½ cups water
> 1 cup vinegar
> 12 whole cloves
> 4 sticks cinnamon
> 1 cup light brown sugar

Cover prunes with the water and soak overnight.
Drain in the morning, reserving water. If there
is not 1½ cups, add enough water to make that
amount. Pack prunes in clean, hot jars. Make
syrup by boiling the reserved water, vinegar,
spices (tied in a cloth bag) and sugar together
for about 10 minutes. Remove spice bag and
pour hot syrup over prunes in jars. Seal at once.
Let stand for 2 months before using. Makes
about 2 pints.

These pickled prunes are wonderful served with meats or poultry.

Simple Chutney

4 pounds ripe tomatoes
5 large onions
5 large tart apples
¼ teaspoon red pepper
1 tablespoon salt
2 cups light brown sugar
2 cups vinegar
1 teaspoon whole pickling spice

Peel tomatoes and apples. Slice apples thin. Peel and dice onions. Combine fruit and vegetables and add vinegar, sugar, red pepper and salt. Cook all very slowly for about 3 hours. Add the pickling spice, tied in a cloth bag, the last 30 minutes of cooking. Discard bag and seal chutney in hot glass jars. Makes 5 to 6 pints.

Beet Relish

4 cups cooked beets, chopped fine
4 cups raw cabbage, chopped fine
½ cup grated horseradish
2 cups sugar
pinch of black pepper
pinch of red pepper
1 cup vinegar
1 cup water

Mix beets, cabbage and horseradish, add sugar

and spices. Bring water and vinegar to boiling point and pour over vegetable mixture. Do not cook, but seal at once in hot glass jars. Let stand 1 month before using. Makes about 5 pints.

This relish is a handsome, dark red color and is especially good served with cold meats.

Sweet Red Pepper Relish

    12 large sweet red peppers
    1 tablespoon salt
    2 cups vinegar
    3 cups sugar

Remove seeds from the peppers, chop and sprinkle with the salt. Let stand overnight. In the morning, drain well, add sugar and vinegar. Simmer very slowly until about as thick as marmalade. Seal in hot jars. Makes about 2 pints. Excellent with cold meats.

Spiced Tomato Relish

    4 pounds ripe tomatoes
    1 sweet red pepper
    3 cups sugar
    2 cups vinegar
    1 teaspoon cinnamon
    1 teaspoon ground cloves
    ½ teaspoon salt

Peel tomatoes and cut up. Remove seeds from red pepper and chop. Add the red pepper to the tomatoes, then add rest of ingredients. Simmer slowly for about 2 hours. Seal at once in hot jars. Makes about 3 pints.

Raw Vegetable Relish

2 large carrots
4 large onions
4 large sweet green peppers
4 large sweet red peppers
1 small cabbage
¼ cup salt
3 cups vinegar
2 cups sugar
1 tablespoon celery seed
1 tablespoon mustard seed
pinch of red pepper

Peel carrots and onions. Remove seeds from the peppers. Chop vegetables fine, or put through coarse knife of food grinder. Sprinkle with the salt and let stand 3 hours. Drain well. Add vinegar, sugar and spices. Mix well and pack into sterile jars, making sure that vegetables are well covered with the liquid. Seal at once. Makes 5 to 6 pints.

This uncooked relish will keep for several months if liquid covers the vegetables well, and jars are kept in a cool place. Store opened jars of relish in the refrigerator.

Corn Relish

5 cups cooked corn, cut from cob
½ cup chopped sweet green pepper
½ cup chopped sweet red pepper
1 cup chopped onion
½ cup chopped celery
1 tablespoon prepared mustard
1 tablespoon mustard seed

2 teaspoons celery seed
½ teaspoon turmeric
1 cup sugar
2 cups vinegar
2 teaspoons salt

Mix all together and simmer very slowly for about 30 minutes. Seal at once in hot jars. Makes about 5 pints.

This flavorful relish was enjoyed many years ago eaten as a sandwich filling with bread and butter. I remember many school lunches when children of the neighborhood brought at least one such sandwich.

Golden Glow Pickle

½ peck ripe yellow cucumbers
6 large onions
3 sweet red peppers
3 sweet green peppers
¼ cup salt
1 teaspoon turmeric
2 cups white sugar
2 cups light brown sugar
1 teaspoon celery seed
1 teaspoon mustard seed
2 cups vinegar

Peel cucumbers, discard seeds and pulp, and dice the firm white inner rind. Peel onions and dice. Remove seeds from the peppers and dice. Cover the diced vegetables with the ¼ cup salt. Stir slightly to mix and let stand overnight. In the morning, drain and rinse in fresh water. Drain again. Combine turmeric, sugars, spice and vinegar and add to vegetable mixture. Cook slowly until cucumber cubes are transparent but not mushy, about 20 minutes. Seal at once in hot jars, covering well with the liquid. Makes about 4 to 5 quarts.

This is a colorful and delicious pickle.

Spicy Pickles

　　1 peck tiny cucumbers
　　½ cup salt for brine
　　2 quarts water for brine
　　4 quarts vinegar
　　11 cups sugar
　　1 ounce stick cinnamon
　　1 ounce whole cloves
　　2 ounces whole mixed pickling spice
　　1 teaspoon alum

Scrub cucumbers well. Soak for 24 hours in a brine made of the ½ cup salt dissolved in the 2 quarts water. Drain cucumbers and cover with boiling water. Drain again and pack at once into hot glass jars. Have ready the mixture of the vinegar, sugar, spices and alum, which has been brought to the boiling point. Pour over the hot cucumbers and seal at once. Makes about 8 quarts.

Ripe Cucumber Pickle

　　8 pounds ripe yellow cucumbers
　　¾ cup salt
　　4 quarts water
　　1 quart vinegar

3 pounds sugar
1 tablespoon whole cloves
1 tablespoon crumbled stick cinnamon

Peel cucumbers and discard seeds and pulp. Cut the firm white inner rind into nice-sized pieces, about 2 x 4 inches. Cover with a brine made of the ¾ cup salt dissolved in the 4 quarts water and let stand overnight. In the morning, drain well. In fresh water, simmer a few slices at a time until they are tender, but be careful not to cook them enough to get mushy. Drain well and pack into sterile glass jars.

Tie spices in a bag and combine with vinegar and sugar. Simmer 30 minutes, then pour hot liquid over packed cucumber slices. Let stand overnight. In the morning, drain off syrup and bring it to boiling again with the spice bag. Simmer 5 minutes, remove spice bag and pour boiling syrup over pickle, filling jars to the top with syrup, and seal at once. This delicious pickle should stand a month before using. Makes 5 to 6 quarts.

Excellent Saccharin Pickles

about 1 peck small cucumbers
1 gallon vinegar
2 tablespoons salt
2 tablespoons dry mustard
2 teaspoons powdered saccharin
about 8 teaspoons whole mixed pickling spice

Scrub cucumbers and pack into sterile glass jars. Add salt, saccharin and mustard to the vinegar, stirring to dissolve dry ingredients. Add 1 tea-spoon whole mixed pickling spice to the top of each quart jar of cucumbers and fill to the top with the cold vinegar mixture. Seal at once and let stand a month before using. Makes about 8 quarts.

Dutch Pickle

2 quarts peeled, sliced medium cucumbers
2 quarts sliced green tomatoes
2 quarts sliced onions
1 large bunch celery, trimmed and sliced thin
6 sweet red peppers, seeded and diced
1 cup salt
2 quarts vinegar
3 pounds sugar
1 cup flour
1 cup dry mustard
1 tablespoon turmeric

Combine vegetables and sprinkle with the 1 cup salt. Let stand overnight. In the morning, scald vegetables in the brine, then drain well. Mix vinegar with the sugar, flour, mustard and tur-meric and bring to the boiling point. Pour over vegetables and simmer for about 30 minutes. Stir frequently and do not allow mixture to boil. Pour into hot glass jars and seal at once. Makes about 6 quarts.

Sweet Dill Pickles

1 peck cucumbers (5- to 6-inch)
about 16 dill sprigs
about 8 garlic cloves

2¾ cups vinegar
5½ cups water
1¾ cups sugar
½ cup salt
about 1 teaspoon alum

Scrub cucumbers well and quarter lengthwise. In bottom of each sterile glass jar place 1 sprig of dill and ½ clove of garlic. Fit in slices of cucumber and top with another sprig of dill and another ½ clove of garlic.

Combine vinegar, water, sugar and salt and bring to boiling. Put a small pinch of alum in top of each jar and fill with the boiling vinegar mixture. Seal at once. Let stand at least 3 weeks before using. Makes about 8 quarts.

Switchel

1 cup light brown sugar
1 cup vinegar
½ cup light molasses
1 tablespoon ground ginger
1 quart cold water

Combine and stir well. While this very old beverage may be chilled in the refrigerator before drinking, it doesn't need chilling to be an effective and refreshing thirst-quencher. In by-gone days on the farms, water pumped from deep in the well was considered quite cold enough for any man.

There are many variations of this drink, some using maple sugar and boiled cider. My grandfather always said that nothing quenched a man's thirst or cooled his dusty throat in haying time so well as this homely drink.

Blackberry Cordial

1 quart blackberry juice
2 cups sugar
½ stick of cinnamon
2 tablespoons whole cloves
¼ ounce allspice
about 1 pint brandy

The blackberry juice may be obtained by simmering about 3 quarts blackberries, crushed, with ½ cup water, watching carefully to guard against scorching. Strain.

To 1 quart of the juice add the 2 cups sugar, ½ stick of cinnamon, 2 tablespoons whole cloves and ¼ ounce allspice. Boil for 20 minutes, then strain again. Add the brandy, 1 pint to each quart of liquid. Bottle.

Index

Apples:
  baked, in maple, 168
  onions, baked with, 74-75;
  roll (maple), 156;
  spareribs, baked with, 37;
  see also Candy; Dumplings;
    Fruitcake; Jelly; Marma-
    lade; Muffins; Pancakes;
    Pie; Pudding, baked

Beans:
  baked, 5, 72;
  green, 42;
  string, 79-80

Beef:
  corned, boiled, 18;
  heart, stuffed, 46;
  liver, 44-45;
  meatballs with gravy, 32;
  meat loaf, spicy, 30;
  oven stew, 27-28;
  pot roast with prunes, 27;
  short ribs, baked, 30;
  stew, with dumplings, 29-
    30;
  tomatoes, baked with, 31;
  tongue, cold boiled, 45-46

Beets, 77-78, 190

Biscuits:
  buttermilk, 94-95;
  cheese (store), 97;
  cinnamon, 97;
  maple, 97, 156;
  marmalade, 97;
  milk (sweet), 96;
  orange tea, 98;
  sour cream, 96;
  sour milk, 96

Bread, yeast:
  Christmas, 87-88;
  cinnamon, 88-89;
  cheese (store), light, 89;
  maple oatmeal, 154-155;
  potato (white), 84-85;
  white, 85-86;

  see also Rolls

Bread, quick:
  apple, 93;
  cottage cheese fruit, 92;
  johnnycake, apple, 100;
  johnnycake, custard, 100;
  maple bran, 153;
  maple brown, 152;
  maple coffee cake, 154;
  maple gingerbread, 155;
  prune, 93-94;
  raisin graham, 94;
  see also Biscuits; Muffins;
    Popovers

Buttermilk, substitute for
  sour milk, ix

Cabbage, 67, 81

Cake:
  chocolate, dark, 113-114;
  chocolate, light potato, 114;
  cream (sweet), 115;
  jam, 119-120;
  maple layer, 158;
  maple sponge, 159;
  maple upsidedown, 159;
  prune, filled, 117-118;
  salt pork, 116-117;
  spice puffs, 113;
  see also Fruitcake; Short-
    cake

Carrots:
  onions, creamed, 75-76;
  see also Marmalade; Pie;
    Pudding, steamed

Candy:
  apple crystals, 178-179;
  caramels, maple, 171;
  chocolates, simple, 177-
    178;
  divinity, maple, 170-171;
  fudge, maple nut, 170;
  fudge, maple chocolate,
    173;
  horehound, 179;

TX
715   Vaughan
.V35   Yankee Hill-country Cooking

DATE D

TX
715   Vaughan
.V35   Yankee Hill-country
        Cooking

DATE	ISSUED TO
DEC 16 '77	Ted Caphell
JAN 25 '78	"
FEB 15 '78	"
NOV 17 '78	
OCT 31 '80	Vonnie Santo
NOV 14 '80	Lucy B
OCT 17 1980	

DEC 16
FEB 15
NOV
OCT
OCT
MAR
OCT 31 '80
NOV 14 '80
OCT 17 1980